Every Teacher
a Leader

Every Teacher a Leader

Developing the Needed Dispositions, Knowledge, and Skills for Teacher Leadership

Barbara B. Levin

Lynne Schrum

A SAGE Publishing Company

FOR INFORMATION:

Corwin

A SAGE Company

2455 Teller Road

Thousand Oaks, California 91320

(800) 233-9936

www.corwin.com

SAGE Publications Ltd.

1 Oliver's Yard

55 City Road

London EC1Y 1SP

United Kingdom

SAGE Publications India Pvt. Ltd.

B 1/I 1 Mohan Cooperative Industrial Area

Mathura Road, New Delhi 110 044

India

SAGE Publications Asia-Pacific Pte. Ltd.

3 Church Street

#10-04 Samsung Hub

Singapore 049483

Library of Congress Cataloging-in-Publication Data

Names: Levin, Barbara B., author. | Schrum, Lynne, author.

Title: Every teacher a leader : developing the needed dispositions, knowledge, and skills for teacher leadership / Barbara B. Levin, Lynne Schrum.

Description: Thousand Oaks, California : Corwin, a Sage Company, [2016] | Includes bibliographical references and index.

Identifiers: LCCN 2016000259 | ISBN 978-1-5063-2643-6 (pbk. : alk. paper)

Subjects: LCSH: Educational leadership—United States. | Teacher participation in administration—United States | Teachers—Professional relationships—United States. | School management and organization—United States.

Classification: LCC LB2805 .L39198 2016 | DDC 371.2—dc23 LC record available at http://lccn.loc.gov/2016000259

This book is printed on acid-free paper.

Acquisitions Editor: Ariel Bartlett

Editorial Assistant: Andrew Olson

Production Editor: Amy Schroller

Copy Editor: Deanna Noga

Typesetter: C&M Digitals (P) Ltd.

Indexer: Robie Grant

Cover Designer: Candice Harman

Marketing Manager: Jill Margulies

16 17 18 19 20 10 9 8 7 6 5 4 3 2 1

Contents

Preface

This preface includes the rationale and purpose for this book, highlights the major themes emphasized throughout, and describes the audiences for whom this book was written. It sets the stage for the concept of teacher leadership, which is so important today, and explains why teacher leaders need to learn and develop the dispositions, knowledge, and skills emphasized in this new book on teacher leadership. It also explains how this book is organized, describes the special features in the book, and details the contents of two online guides for this book—one for teacher leaders and one for school and district leaders.

According to the research literature, ongoing, high-quality professional development (PD) is a key for developing and sustaining teacher leaders (Copeland & Gray, 2002; Crawford, Roberts, & Hickmann, 2010; Jackson, Burrus, Barrett, & Roberts, 2010), so this book provides the content needed to support professional learning focused on teacher leadership. York-Barr and Duke (2004) found that teacher leaders grow in their understanding of instructional, professional, and organizational practice as they lead. To support every teacher in becoming an effective leader, the content in this book is useful for both prospective and current teacher leaders, whether they have formal or informal roles and responsibilities as teacher leaders.

WHAT IS THE RATIONALE FOR THIS BOOK?

Current books about teacher leadership address this topic rather generically, or they are actually about developing school leaders (e.g., principals, assistant principals, department chairs), not other opportunities for teacher leadership. Therefore, one goal of this book is to address specific dispositions, knowledge, and skills needed by teacher leaders. It is one thing to understand what teacher leadership is all about, which we discuss in the opening chapters, but quite another thing to learn what is needed to become an effective teacher leader. This is our rationale for offering a content- and skills-driven book about teacher leadership for those who want to become teacher leaders, learn more about teacher leadership, or for school or district leaders who wish to help others develop the needed dispositions, knowledge, and skills for successful teacher leadership. Therefore, the audience for this book includes current and future teacher leaders as well as current and future school and district leaders. It is our strong belief that both groups must understand the complexity, challenges, and benefits of strong partnerships between administrators and teachers if our schools are to be as successful as possible. Another audience includes higher education faculty who are preparing future teacher leaders, as well as future school leaders who will be ready to embrace and leverage teacher leadership in their schools.

Successful teacher leaders can make positive differences in their schools and districts by taking on many important roles and responsibilities—either formally or informally. No single administrator can manage everything needed in today's schools on his or her own. Encouraging teacher leaders to contribute to the good of the whole leads to a positive school culture because everybody is working together. Therefore, another rationale for this book is to advocate for teacher leadership and to help prepare more teachers to take on leadership roles. When this is accomplished, we believe school and district leaders will see a change in both culture and productivity because teacher leaders are active in helping improve education for all children. Ultimately, we believe increased opportunities for teacher leadership will lead to better teacher retention, which ultimately benefits both learners and teachers as well as school and district leaders and the wider community.

WHAT IS THE PURPOSE OF THIS BOOK?

Our intention is to broaden and deepen the concept of teacher leadership by detailing what teacher leaders can and should know and be able to do. In doing so, our goal is to empower current and future teacher leaders! We accomplish this by articulating and elaborating the dispositions, knowledge, and skills that teacher leaders need to learn and be able to do to survive and thrive in today's schools. Our assumption is that individuals are not necessarily born to be leaders, and certainly not genetically programmed; further, they do not have to be designated by "others" to lead! Instead we believe that teacher leaders can learn how to lead with encouragement, new knowledge, skill building, guidance, and encouragement as they find their niche—first in their classroom, then in their school, and ultimately in their district, community, and beyond. In other words, the main purpose of this book is to share what teachers should learn so they can develop into successful teacher leaders, because we believe that every teacher can be a leader.

Teacher leaders can learn how to lead with encouragement, new knowledge, skill building, guidance, and encouragement as they find their niche—first in their classroom, then in their school, and ultimately in their district, community, and beyond.

The teacher leadership literature reports that advocacy, empathy, questioning, vision creating, collaboration and networking, which we advocate, should characterize teacher leaders' skills. The literature also says teacher leaders must be disposed to take risks, be persistent, challenge existing practices, feel a sense of efficacy, and be resilient (Katzenmeyer & Moller, 2009). We agree that these and other dispositions are important for teacher leaders to display. For these reasons, this book not only identifies specific knowledge and skills that teacher leaders need to develop, but it also addresses the dispositions needed by teacher leaders if they are going to be successful.

In our experience working with teacher leaders, we see that many teachers think leadership is not about them, or not for them. They think that if they have not yet been appointed to formal positions as grade level or department chairs, or are not currently serving on their school improvement committee, they are not teacher leaders. Many teachers we know simply feel they do not yet have enough experience to be considered a leader, although we do not equate leadership with years of experience. In other words, some teachers fear that others will not acknowledge them as leaders because they are not veteran teachers or have not been formally named to leadership positions. Other teachers are stymied because the roles and responsibilities of teacher leaders are typically ill defined, are not always recognized, and in the past have not always been supported by formal leaders in their schools and districts—principals, curriculum facilitators, department chairs, lead teachers, and so on. Conversely, many teacher leaders are asked to lead without any formal skill development about aspects of leadership that they want and need to take on leadership roles (Katzenmeyer & Moller, 2009; York-Barr & Duke, 2004). This book provides those skills, as well as the knowledge base and dispositions needed by teacher leaders, because we believe that *teacher leaders can make a real difference in schools today.*

WHAT ARE THE MAJOR THEMES OF THIS BOOK?

The title of this book encompasses our major themes: *Every Teacher a Leader: Developing the Needed Dispositions, Knowledge, and Skills for Teacher Leadership.* The overarching theme for this book is "every teacher a leader" because we strongly believe that every teacher can be a leader. Related themes include the dispositions, knowledge, and skills needed to be a successful teacher leader. Dispositions are those needed by teacher leaders who are inclined to act as one who is ethical, self-efficacious, positive, flexible, supportive, caring, and a risk taker, among others. Skills needed by teacher leaders are those often considered to be soft skills or people skills. The skill-based themes in this book include the importance of good communication, relationship building, collaboration, teamwork, problem solving, critical thinking, and conflict resolution, among others. Much of what teacher leaders need to learn stems from self-knowledge, which makes the development of metacognitive thinking another theme in this book. A final theme is that a teacher leader is not something one is; rather, teacher leadership is something that can be

> *Becoming a teacher leader is not something one is, but something that can be learned.*

learned. In other words, teacher leadership is not a personality trait. Leadership, we believe, can be developed by acquiring new knowledge, practicing new skills, and exercising appropriate dispositions.

WHO SHOULD READ THIS BOOK?

The content of this book is straightforward, practical, and immediately applicable to anyone wanting to be a successful teacher leader or hoping to encourage teachers to become teacher leaders. The audiences for this book include teachers who seek leadership roles, professional development leaders, school and district administrators, and teacher preparation faculty. All these groups have a stake in developing teachers as leaders at either the in-service or preservice level.

Professional educators responsible for professional learning can use this book as a resource for planning their own efforts to develop teacher leaders and/or as a textbook for groups of teachers to work through as they learn to become teacher leaders. School and district administrators can use it to better understand what it takes to foster teacher leadership in their schools and districts. Then they can recommend this book to their department chairs, team leaders, Professional Learning Community (PLC) leaders, curriculum facilitators, and lead teachers for their own professional learning. School and district leaders may also use it as a book club selection for groups of current or prospective teacher leaders learning more about teacher leadership either within a school or across schools in a district.

Teachers, both novice and experienced, who are interested in leadership will find this book very readable and will benefit from the content knowledge and skills, as well as the scenarios, activities, self-assessments, and the many reflection and discussion questions included in this book. While teachers may read this book on their own, we suggest sharing it with other potential teacher leaders in their schools because it can be a catalyst for thoughtful discussions. With this in mind, teachers in PLCs could use this book as a source for both discussion and action.

This book can be used in college and university courses for teachers and administrators, including the growing number of postsecondary institutions developing degrees and certificates in teacher leadership in both online and face-to-face formats. Teacher education faculty will find this book to be an ideal textbook for classes about teacher leadership at either the preservice or in-service level. Another audience for this book is university-based leadership faculty who can recommend this book as a supplementary textbook or a book club choice for current and future leaders—principals, assistant principals, central office personnel, and superintendents. This book will be especially valuable in programs that espouse transformative, distributed, or instructional leadership, as discussed in Chapters 1 and 2. Another audience for this book is alternative licensure programs such as Teach for America that prepare their recruits to be teacher leaders from the very start. We are also hopeful that state departments of education will consider more formal recognition of teachers as leaders through certification or other formal ways after reading this book.

HOW IS THIS BOOK ORGANIZED?

Chapter 1 begins with definitions of teacher leadership and a brief history of the four waves of teacher leadership. Models for school leadership are defined and connected to teacher leadership. Examples of how teachers are currently leading are provided, and the kinds of roles and responsibilities that teacher leaders take up either formally or informally are included. The research base for teacher leadership is covered briefly, and the Teacher Leadership Model Standards are included (see www.teacherleaderstandards.org).

Chapter 2 addresses how we can and should develop and promote teacher leadership. Best practice and models of leadership, mentoring, and coaching that support teacher leaders are described. We also identify obstacles that hinder successful teacher leadership as well as what supports teacher leadership today. To address the constraints on teacher leadership, we include ways to engage and reward teacher leaders.

Chapter 3 focuses on dispositions, ways to establish a vision and goals, and assessing readiness and self-efficacy for teacher leadership. Several opportunities for personal assessment and self-analysis are included in this chapter. Activities, scenarios, and additional resources are included for this and every chapter in the online guides for this book. These are offered to help readers reflect on the dispositions, visions, and goals needed for teacher leadership.

Chapters 4 and 5 address the knowledge base needed by teacher leaders. Chapter 4 focuses on the kinds of self-knowledge teacher leaders need and ways to help teacher leaders uncover important knowledge about themselves. Other basic knowledge includes understanding adult learners and their needs and knowing how teachers develop throughout their careers. In addition, understanding how teachers can develop metacognitive thinking about teacher leadership is also important knowledge addressed in this chapter.

Chapter 5 addresses additional kinds of knowledge that teacher leaders need to have about schools and districts as systems and knowledge about education policy. We also discuss why knowledge of culturally responsive parent involvement is also important knowledge for teacher leaders. How to conduct teacher research, which is crucially important for developing as a teacher leader, is introduced in this chapter and extended with a step-by-step account of how to conduct teacher action research in Appendix B. Additional activities, scenarios, and resources to help readers reflect on and practice the knowledge base needed for teacher leadership are found in the online companion guides.

Chapters 6 and 7 address numerous skills needed by teacher leaders. Chapter 6 addresses core interpersonal skills: communication, group facilitation, time management, digital literacy, and conflict resolution. Chapter 7 focuses on additional interpersonal skills as teachers take on roles and responsibilities related to leading professional development, writing grants, and advocating for their fellow teachers and education as a profession. Activities, scenarios, and additional resources to help readers reflect on and exercise skills needed for teacher leadership are found in online guides for teachers and teacher leaders and for school and district leaders.

Chapter 8 includes information about the future of teacher leadership and projections about what schools full of teacher leaders could accomplish. Suggestions for how school and district leaders can support teacher leadership are included in this chapter. In addition, two potential agendas with suggested activities for professional learning opportunities around teacher leadership are provided.

Three appendices complete the book. Appendices A and C can be used for self-evaluation and to gather data from others about readiness for teacher leadership. Appendix B is a step-by-step guide to conducting teacher action research, which we think is a key activity with which teacher leaders should be engaged.

WHAT SPECIAL FEATURES ARE IN THIS BOOK?

Special features embedded in this book include several self-evaluations, lists of information, tips for teacher leaders, and numerous suggestions for activities to practice the dispositions, knowledge, and skills that teacher leaders need to develop. All chapters include an opening dialogue written from the point of view of a teacher leader beginning to think about teacher leadership and a school leader seeking to promote teacher leadership. Quotes from teacher leaders we have worked with are included to provide authentic voices of teachers who were learning to be teacher leaders or already leading in their classrooms and schools.

The companion website for this book hosts two guides, which are provided for those working with teachers who want to be leaders. One guide contains activities for current or future teacher leaders to use, and the other is for school and district leaders who are mentoring teacher leaders. These guides include all the activities described in the chapters as well as additional activities, questions for reflection and discussion, supplemental readings, scenarios to discuss, and copies of various self-assessment surveys in the book. The self-assessment surveys from Appendix A and C are duplicated in these guides, and permission is granted to duplicate these and any of these materials in these guides to use with anyone striving to be a strong teacher leader. (See https://resources.corwin.com/everyteacheraleader.)

Publisher's Acknowledgments

Corwin gratefully acknowledges the editorial insight and guidance of the following reviewers:

Elizabeth Alvarez
Principal
Chicago Public Schools
Chicago, IL

Cortney Crews
English Teacher
Hunters Lane High School
Nashville, TN

Susan N. Imamura
Principal, Retired
Manoa Elementary School
Honolulu, HI

Sue Kessler
Executive Principal
Metro Nashville Public Schools
Hunters Lane High School
Nashville, TN

About the Authors

Barbara B. Levin has been a professor in the Department of Teacher Education and Higher Education at the University of North Carolina at Greensboro (UNCG) since 1993. She was an elementary school teacher for 17 years before earning her PhD at the University of California-Berkeley. Dr. Levin served as the Director of the Teachers Academy at UNCG, assistant department chair, and director of graduate studies. She was awarded the first Mentoring-Advising-Supervising (MAS) Award in the School of Education at UNCG. Dr. Levin also served as an Associate Editor for *Teacher Education Quarterly* for 8 years, and was co-PI on a 5-year, $1.4 million National Professional Development grant from the Department of Education called TESOL for ALL. Her research interests include: understanding how teachers' pedagogical beliefs develop across their careers; case-based teaching; problem-based learning (PBL); universal design for learning (UDL); and leading, teaching, and learning with technology. Dr. Levin has published eight books and over 40 articles in well-respected research journals.

Lynne Schrum is Dean of the Abraham S. Fischler College of Education at Nova Southeastern University, Ft. Lauderdale, FL. Previously, she was the Dean of the College of Education and Human Services at West Virginia University. Prior to that, she was a professor and coordinator of elementary education in the College of Education and Human Development at George Mason University. Her research and teaching focus on preparing teachers for the 21st century, appropriate uses of information technology, and leadership in a digital world. She has written 11 books and numerous articles on these subjects; the most recent is *How 2, Web 2: How to for Educators*. Schrum served on AERA's Council, was editor of the *Journal of Research on Technology in Education (JRTE)* (2002–2012), and is a past president of the International Society for Technology in Education (ISTE).

CHAPTER 1

Why Teacher Leadership?

> *The hope for teacher leadership is continuous improvement of teaching and learning in our nation's schools, with the result being increased achievement for every student.*
>
> (York-Barr & Duke, 2004, p. 255)

VIEW FROM A SCHOOL LEADER	VIEW FROM A TEACHER LEADER
Mrs. Brown, I would like to talk with you about taking on more leadership in the school this year. I think you have shown a lot of leadership in your PLC, so I would like you to do that on a larger scale and to assist me in accomplishing our shared goals. I think you can be a teacher leader in our school.	*Mr. Peterson, I am not sure I even know what it takes to be a teacher leader, but I am honored you think of me as one! What does that mean, exactly? I am not sure I have the knowledge or skills needed, but I suppose it depends on what you want me to do in addition to teaching my students.*

To provide some background about teacher leadership, this chapter begins with several definitions and a brief history of teacher leadership. We also discuss contemporary leadership styles and how they relate to teacher leadership. Examples of how teachers are currently leading are described, as well as examples of the kinds of roles and responsibilities that teacher leaders can accomplish either formally or informally. The research base for teacher leadership is addressed briefly, and the Teacher Leadership Model Standards are provided. Additional activities that will help you think more about teacher leadership are also provided. Specific questions answered in this chapter include:

1. How is teacher leadership currently defined?

2. How might teacher leadership be defined?

3. Why do we need teacher leaders?

4. What kinds of roles and responsibilities can teachers take on formally and informally?

5. What leadership styles support teacher leadership?

HOW IS TEACHER LEADERSHIP CURRENTLY DEFINED?

Teacher leadership has been defined in recent years as a process, a set of actions, and by specific activities that teachers undertake as leaders. Teacher leadership also has been characterized by verbs that convey actions teachers do as leaders to influence, improve, increase, contribute, mentor, model, share, and accept responsibility. Over a decade ago, York-Barr & Duke (2004) reviewed the research literature and defined teacher leadership in the following way:

> After reflecting on the literature as a whole, we suggest that teacher leadership is the process by which teachers, individually or collectively, influence their colleagues, principals, and other members of school communities to improve teaching and learning practices with the aim of increased student learning and achievement. Such leadership work involves three intentional development foci: individual development, collaboration or team development, and organizational development. (pp. 287–288)

Describing specific actions, Ackerman and Mackenzie (2006) stated, "Teachers lead informally by revealing their classroom practice, sharing their expertise, asking questions of colleagues, mentoring new teachers, and modeling how teachers collaborate on issues of practice" (p. 66). Katzenmeyer & Moller (2009) have also defined teacher leadership by the actions that teacher leaders undertake: "Teacher leaders lead within and beyond the classroom; identify with and contribute to a community of teacher learners and leaders; influence others toward improved educational practice; and accept responsibility for achieving the outcomes of their leadership" (p. 6). We concur with these definitions of teacher leadership. However, we aim to both broaden and deepen the concept of teacher leadership throughout this book by detailing the dispositions, knowledge, and skills needed for successful teacher leadership.

ACTIVITY: First, THINK about and then write down your own definition of teacher leadership. This might include the process of teacher leadership as well as the actions and activities of teacher leaders. Second, PAIR up with one or two others to share your definition, and to COMPARE the similarities and differences in your definitions. Third, SHARE with the whole group, and listen for similarities and differences in your definitions. Fourth, try to come to a CONSENSUS definition of teacher leadership that the whole group feels comfortable with. Finally, COMPARE your group's consensus definition with how several "experts" have defined teacher leadership.

NOTE: You can find a list of teacher leadership definitions written by some of the experts on p. 10 in Jackson, Burrus, Barrett, and Roberts, 2010 (available at www.ets.org/Media/Research/pdf/RR-10-27.pdf).

The way teacher leadership operates in schools has evolved in four waves during the past few decades (Bradley-Levine, 2011; Hatch, White & Faigenbaum, 2005; Little, 2003). In the first wave, teacher leaders were only those with formal roles such as department chair or grade-level chair, a role the principal typically awarded to senior members of the faculty. In the second wave, other formal leadership positions emerged for some teachers, such as curriculum facilitator or lead teacher. However, these leadership roles usually meant that teachers had to leave their classrooms to take on schoolwide or district-level positions. In the third wave, teacher leadership included more collegial support roles with teachers serving, for example, as mentors or advisors. These kinds of leadership roles, whether formally assigned or done informally, allowed teachers to remain in their classrooms. This shift from previously more administrative and authoritative roles assigned to teacher leaders led to more opportunities and different kinds of leadership roles, such as membership on leadership teams and hiring committees. This in turn led to the current and fourth wave of teacher leadership, which is a manifestation of distributed leadership (cf. Harris, 2003; Mayrowetz, 2008; Murphy, Smylieb, Mayrowetz, & Louis, 2009; Spillane, 2005).

Today, teacher leaders may lead formally by taking on assigned roles or lead informally by speaking about their classroom practices, sharing their expertise, asking questions of colleagues, mentoring new teachers, and modeling how teachers can collaborate on issues of practice (Ackerman & Mackenzie, 2006; Raffanti, 2008). A new vision for teacher leaders who are called teacherpreneurs (Berry, Byrd, & Wieder, 2013) may herald a fifth wave of teacher leadership for those who both remain in the classroom part-time and take on various leadership and advocacy roles outside their classrooms part-time.

HOW MIGHT TEACHER LEADERSHIP BE DEFINED?

We are advocates for both fourth- and fifth-wave teacher leadership, including taking on a hybrid of leadership roles both inside and outside the classroom, so we focus on the knowledge, skills, and dispositions needed to make this possible for any teacher who desires formal or informal leadership opportunities. A *teacherpreneur*, for example, is defined as "a classroom expert who still teaches while finding time, space, and (ideally) much-deserved reward for spreading both sound pedagogical practices and policy ideas" (Berry et al., 2013, p. xvii). However, we know that many potential teacher leaders do not want to leave their classrooms or schools and that the needed supports and structures for teacherpreneurs are just beginning. Also, we do not see teacher leadership as a trait, or only for those who have formal titles such as curriculum facilitator, lead teacher, grade-level chair, or department chair. Instead, we define *teacher leaders* as those who lead in various formal and informal ways in their classrooms, schools, districts, and communities. They may become teacherpreneurs, but they may not. In fact, we believe there is no one best way to characterize teacher leaders and that every teacher can be a leader.

> We define teacher leaders as those who lead in various formal and informal ways in their classrooms, schools, districts, and communities.

We do think teacher leaders should first and foremost be instructional leaders in their classrooms. We also believe that all teachers can and should lead both formally and informally in multiple ways in their schools, districts, and professional organizations, although we do not set a time limit for this to develop. We believe teachers can and should be defined as leaders when they share their knowledge and experience with other teachers, lead professional learning opportunities, serve on ad hoc or formal committees and task forces, and work with parents and families. In sum, we think teacher leaders should be recognized as leaders when they serve their profession in a variety of ways—including, but not limited to serving as models for preservice teachers and as mentors for beginning teachers. These are but a few of the ways teachers can and do demonstrate leadership, which we expand on and develop throughout this chapter and the remainder of this book.

A major theme in this book is that every teacher can learn and develop into a teacher leader. We have seen this happen time and time again with both novice and experienced teachers when they are challenged to take on leadership projects, conduct action research in their classrooms, understand how others lead in formal and informal ways, and when they learn about and reflect on what teacher leadership is all about. For example, one teacher wrote the following at the end of her teacher leadership course:

> *A valuable lesson about teacher leadership that I gained is that teachers are resources. So many of my own colleagues have ideas like I do and when we work together to share those, our school is a better place. Often teachers become like islands in their own classrooms, not venturing out to see what works for anyone else. We are stronger pedagogically when we learn from one another. Listening to teachers share about what worked for them, and sharing what worked for me, was an encouraging time for everyone.* (Emily, 2015)

In Table 1.1, we share a list of knowledge, skills, and dispositions needed by teacher leaders that was constructed by a recent group of teacher leaders we worked with. While the items in each column are not exhaustive, they foreshadow much of what this book addresses.

TABLE 1.1 Knowledge, Skills, and Dispositions Needed for Teacher Leadership

KNOWLEDGE	SKILLS	DISPOSITIONS
• Curriculum and content	• Listening	• Flexible
• What students need to know at each grade level—vertical alignment	• Communication	• Open
	• Collaboration	• Caring
• School environment	• Time management	• Driven
• Research-based teaching practices	• Organization	• Supportive
	• People skills (e.g., relationship building)	• Determination
• What's new and current in education	• Problem solving	• Cheerful
• Knowledge of people—how people think, learn, interact	• Engaging others	• Consistent
	• Public speaking	• Positive
• Knowledge of the school community—parents, staff, and students	• Facilitating meetings	• Approachable
	• Data analysis	• Active
• Assessment design		• Patient
• How to interpret and make use of assessment data		• Persistent
		• Tactful
		• Self-efficacious
		• Ethical

ACTIVITY: As an individual or in a group, develop your own list of knowledge, skills, and dispositions that you think are needed for teacher leadership. Alternatively, add to the lists in Table 1.1. Now, prioritize your lists of needed knowledge skills, and dispositions, based on what is realistic or what is most needed in your workplace. Then make a list of the knowledge, skills, and dispositions you personally possess and bring with you as assets into the realm of teacher leadership. Also make a list of needed or desired knowledge, skills, and dispositions that you personally wish to develop to become a successful teacher leader.

WHY DO WE NEED TEACHER LEADERS?

We need teacher leaders today because no one person can possibly accomplish everything needed to run a school well. The job is too complex for a single leader of a school or district, no matter the size. Most school and district leaders understand both the necessity and the value of distributed leadership. In fact, Spillane, Halverson, and Diamond (2001) suggested that to understand leadership, it is important to look beyond what one person can do, or knows how to do, and to look instead at what each person brings to the task, to build on strengths and to tackle issues collaboratively. This includes teacher leaders. And, as Lieberman (2011) wisely noted

> Teachers who become leaders are in a unique position to make change happen. They have learned a great deal about how to teach well and know how to build the kind of school and classroom conditions that can help transform schools. They have not only "been there," but they also have successfully worked with all kinds of students and have learned how to facilitate adult learning as well. They have learned to teach well in the context of a classroom and have developed the kind of knowledge that teachers trust and believe. (p. 16)

Another reason we need teacher leaders is that they can and should be actively involved in any initiatives for improving student achievement. Teacher leaders are needed whenever the goal is to address any problem of practice or other issue in the school. We state the obvious here, because we know if real change or improvement is going to occur, those on the front line who are directly responsible for students need to be involved. After all, they can make or break new initiatives, so their expertise and buy-in are important. In fact, as Angelle (2007) reported, "Teacher leaders who are deprived of the ability to make decisions on what they perceive are critical issues report greater dissatisfaction with their job, more stress, and less loyalty to their principal" (p. 59).

We concur, and we would emphasize that teacher leaders should never work alone—any more than their school leaders should try to go it alone. Nevertheless, principals and even superintendents certainly play important roles by supporting or hindering teacher leadership (Collinson & Cook, 2004; Katzenmeyer & Moller, 2009; Raffanti, 2008). In fact, building relationships and collaborating with others are two key aspects of teacher leadership.

> Collaborative leaders recognize that in today's schools, one person cannot adequately address the needs of all members of the school community. Empowering others to lead alongside the principal builds collegiality and shares opportunities for active participation in the improvement of the school. (Angelle, 2007, p. 55)

Further, without a positive climate for shared decision making and governance, and without understanding the value of distributed leadership, teacher leadership will not take hold, even though we know that opportunities for teacher leadership lead to teacher retention and higher satisfaction among teachers (Angelle, 2007; Katzenmeyer & Moller, 2009; York-Barr & Duke, 2004). As

Lieberman (2011) reminds us, "Without teachers providing collegial leadership, there will be
little improvement in schools. With teacher
leaders, there will be collaborative, facultative,
and ongoing teacher transformation" (p. 18).
In other words, when teachers feel their voices
are heard, their efforts are recognized, and they
have a vested interest in their school, they will be much more likely to stay in
the profession.

> *When teachers feel their voices are heard, their efforts are recognized, and that they have a vested interest in their school, they will be much more likely to stay in the profession.*

In addition, Phelps (2008) has argued that helping teachers become leaders
involves the cultivation of certain knowledge, skills, and dispositions; we certainly agree with this. However, over the years there have been several impediments to teacher leadership, including the fact that teachers are overworked,
frequently underpaid, their time for additional duties is finite, our current
accountability system discourages innovation, and we typically do not reward
teacher leadership-type activities. The lack of support for teacher leaders by
other teachers is also a documented problem in many places (cf. Angelle, 2007;
Danielson, 2006; Katzenmeyer & Moller, 2009; Little, 2003). And because
many teachers perceive that they lack leadership skills, this may constrain many
from taking on leadership roles (Hanuscin, Rebello, & Sinha, 2012; Helterbran,
2010; Katzenmeyer & Moller, 2009). All these issues persist today, but we also
know that today's schools cannot survive, and certainly cannot thrive, unless
everyone is on board and leading together—both school leaders and teacher
leaders.

WHAT KINDS OF ROLES AND RESPONSIBILITIES CAN TEACHERS TAKE ON FORMALLY AND INFORMALLY?

In a review of the teacher leadership literature, Raffanti (2008) identified three
key areas relevant to understanding the roles and experiences of teacher leaders:
context, skills, and challenges. We think these are important considerations
because while teacher leaders can do all the things described in Table 1.2, they
need to consider the context and their personal situation to be sure: (a) their
efforts will be appreciated and supported; (b) they have the skills to do the
things they want to contribute to the school, the organization, or the profession;
and (c) they have the time and energy to take on challenges that may occur
while they are leading. As one of our teacher leaders, Ashley, wisely wrote in her
journal, "*Of course you want to have a supportive school, community, and county, but
you also want to make sure that you can juggle all of the responsibilities without
wearing yourself thin.*"

This book is designed to help teacher leaders consider factors they need to develop so that they will be successful, feel successful, and not give up or burn out as a result of undertaking teacher leadership roles—either formally or informally. What it takes to facilitate and nurture teacher leaders may be somewhat idiosyncratic for each person, but we believe there are some common factors that support and challenge teacher leaders. In our work with teacher leaders, we found they often take on many roles and responsibilities mentioned in the Teacher Leadership Model Standards (see Table 1.2) related to

- Advocating for students
- Mentoring new teachers
- Informing others—sharing their knowledge
- Connecting with the community
- Connecting with parents and families
- Teaching others
- Communicating—being a voice, sharing experiences
- Collaborating with others

Examples of some of the many teacher leadership roles our students have engaged in can be seen in Table 1.2.

ACTIVITY: Reflect on and share the many kinds of leadership roles you have taken on in your life, both inside and outside school. This can include what you are currently doing and what you may have done in the past that could be considered leadership. Look at the list in Table 1.2 again. You should start to notice that there are many things you already do that are examples of teacher leadership! Keep in mind that this list is not exhaustive; it can be expanded, or you may create your own list from scratch with other teacher leaders.

We have relatively new Teacher Leadership Model Standards that can be used to further define teacher leadership (see www.teacherleaderstandards.org). An organization of educators, the Teacher Leadership Exploratory Consortium (2012), developed these standards. This group included union representatives, teachers, school administrators, policy organizations, and leaders in higher education. This consortium was sponsored by a wide range of stakeholders including the Center for Teaching Quality (CTQ), American Federation of Teachers (AFT), Educational Testing Service (ETS), the Education Commission of the States, National Education Association (NEA), and the University of Phoenix. Their goal was to generate dialogue about teacher leadership including the

TABLE 1.2   Examples of the Roles and Responsibilities of Teacher Leaders

EXAMPLES OF INSTRUCTIONAL LEADERSHIP	EXAMPLES OF ORGANIZATIONAL LEADERSHIP	EXAMPLES OF PROFESSIONAL LEADERSHIP
• Developing informal and/or benchmark assessments • Tutoring students • Developing instructional units • Developing question sets for leveled books • Mentoring new teachers • Trying out a new program, strategy, technology, or teaching method • Mentoring preservice teachers • Arranging for field trips or guest speakers • Organizing a service learning project • Mentoring a senior's graduation project • Leading a Friday "special" club • Writing a grant for a special project for new materials • Volunteering to teach an online class • Conducting model lessons • Inviting teachers into your classroom to observe • Undertaking the National Board for Professional Teaching Standards (NBPTS) process	• Leading PLC meetings • Serving as grade-level or department chair • Coaching student groups/clubs/sports • Attending parent-teacher organization meetings • Interviewing potential new administrators or teachers • Organizing a special event—author visit, field day, science fair, book sale, etc. • Evaluating writing or other benchmark tests • Serving on the textbook selection committee • Developing the class schedule • Starting a book club • Organizing or reorganizing the book room, math manipulatives, etc. • Fund raising and/or soliciting donations from business partners • Maintaining the school's website • Starting a version of Japanese Lesson Study, or a peer coaching/peer mentoring collaborative • Serving as a lead teacher, curriculum facilitator, or reading or math coach	• Serving on district or state committees—assessment, textbooks, technology, etc. • Being a union representative • Presenting at conferences • Participating in district-level orientations for new teachers, PD, curriculum revision groups, etc. • Joining online teacher advocacy groups such as The Center for Teaching Quality • Blogging about issues related to teaching • Writing articles or books to share your expertise • Advocating for the profession by writing letters or being active on Twitter or TeacherTube • Developing a website to share ideas with other teachers • Presenting webinars for a professional organization like SimpleK12 or Growth Models • Posting videotapes online to share your teaching with new teachers and teacher education programs

knowledge, skills, and competencies teachers need to become leaders in their schools, districts, and the profession. This consortium compared the standards for teacher leaders with the Interstate School Leaders Licensure Consortium (ISLLC) standards for school leaders and the revised Interstate Teacher Assessment and Standards Consortium (InTASC) standards for teachers. The Teacher Leadership Model Standards include seven domains that encompass critical dimensions of teacher leadership. As can be seen in Table 1.3, each domain includes actions and expectations of teacher leadership in that domain.

TABLE 1.3   Teacher Leader Model Standards

Domain I: Fostering a Collaborative Culture to Support Educator Development and Student Learning.	The teacher leader is well versed in adult learning theory and uses that knowledge to create a community of collective responsibility within his or her school. In promoting this collaborative culture among fellow teachers, administrators, and other school leaders, the teacher leader ensures improvement in educator instruction and, consequently, student learning.
Domain II: Accessing and Using Research to Improve Practice and Student Learning.	The teacher leader keeps abreast of the latest research about teaching effectiveness and student learning, and implements best practices where appropriate. He or she models the use of systematic inquiry as a critical component of teachers' ongoing learning and development.
Domain III: Promoting Professional Learning for Continuous Improvement.	The teacher leader understands that the processes of teaching and learning are constantly evolving. The teacher leader designs and facilitates job-embedded professional development opportunities that are aligned with school improvement goals.
Domain IV: Facilitating Improvements in Instruction and Student Learning.	The teacher leader possesses a deep understanding of teaching and learning, and models an attitude of continuous learning and reflective practice for colleagues. The teacher leader works collaboratively with fellow teachers to constantly improve instructional practices.
Domain V: Promoting the Use of Assessments and Data for School and District Improvement.	The teacher leader is knowledgeable about the design of assessments, both formative and summative. He or she works with colleagues to analyze data and interpret results to inform goals and to improve student learning.
Domain VI: Improving Outreach and Collaboration With Families and Community.	The teacher leader understands the impact that families, cultures, and communities have on student learning. As a result, the teacher leader seeks to promote a sense of partnership among these different groups toward the common goal of excellent education.
Domain VII: Advocating for Student Learning and the Profession.	The teacher leader understands the landscape of education policy and can identify key players at the local, state, and national levels. The teacher leader advocates for the teaching profession and for policies that benefit student learning.

SOURCE: Teacher Leader Model Standards at www.teacherleaderstandards.org. Used with permission of The Center for Teaching Quality.

> ACTIVITY: Unpack the Teacher Leader Model Standards in Table 1.3 by reflecting on and then discussing: (a) what each of these standards looks like in practice, (b) an example of how you may already be enacting one or more of these dimensions of teacher leadership, and then (c) use these standards to set goals for yourself as a teacher leader.

In addition to the Model Teacher Leadership Standards, it is important to note that several states (e.g., Arkansas, California, Connecticut, Georgia, Kansas, Illinois, Louisiana, Kansas, and Tennessee) have established criteria for teacher leaders with the goal of "endorsing, certifying, or credentialing teacher leaders" (Jackson et al., 2010, p. 9). Furthermore, several colleges and universities are using state or national teacher leader standards to develop various types of teacher leadership programs. In fact, more and more states, as well as individual colleges and universities, are preparing both new and experienced teachers as leaders.

Schools and districts are doing the same, which is one reason why we wrote this book—to support teachers seeking to develop themselves as teacher leaders and for others who want to support their development.

WHAT LEADERSHIP STYLES SUPPORT TEACHER LEADERSHIP?

Related to supporting teacher leaders and establishing standards for teacher leadership, it is important to mention three leadership styles we believe are conducive to and supportive of teacher leadership: transformational leadership, distributed leadership, and instructional leadership. We mention these because we understand that the context for supporting teacher leadership will vary according to the leadership style of the administrator(s) in each school and district. As Harris (2003) stated,

> Whatever specific definition of teacher leadership one chooses to adopt, it is clear that its emphasis upon collective action, empowerment and shared agency is reflected in distributed leadership theory. Teacher leadership is centrally and exclusively concerned with the idea that all organisational members can lead and that leadership is a form of agency that be distributed or shared. (p. 317)

For example, the best features recommended by those who advocate for *transformational leadership* (e.g., Bass & Riggio, 2008) include building confidence and trust and being a role model (known as *idealized influence*) and motivating people to work together to achieve a shared vision and to solve problems in an organization without fear of criticism or reprisal (known as *intellectual stimulation*). Transformational leaders have a clear vision, encourage others to see meaning in their work, and challenge them to meet high standards (known as *inspirational motivation*). They also encourage others to take an active role in the organization's culture and climate. Transformational leaders also treat people as unique individuals with specific knowledge and talents and help them succeed (known as *individualized consideration*). Although transformational leadership has been criticized because some espousing this leadership style may be perceived as manipulative or narcissistic, the main characteristics of transformational leadership are a good fit for promoting and supporting teacher leaders. We make this claim because in its ideal form transformational leaders help develop others to become leaders.

Those who enact *distributive leadership* practices are also highly likely to be supportive of teacher leadership because they know that leadership is not about one person working alone and that authentic change flows not only from the top down, but also in all directions. Distributive leadership acknowledges that leadership is a set of interactive, interdependent practices and "a system of practice comprised of a collection of interacting components: leaders, followers, and situation. These three interacting components must be understood together because the system is more than the sum of the component parts or practices" (Spillane, 2005, p. 150). As an example, Spillane (2005) described a study in which distributed leadership in one school was manifested in the reciprocity and interdependence among many leaders when the goal was to improve literacy instruction:

> The principal emphasizes goals and standards, keeps the meetings moving, summarizes comments, and reminds participants of what is expected in their classrooms. The literacy coordinator identifies problems with literacy instruction, suggests solutions and resources, and encourages teachers to present their ideas. The teacher leader describes his or her efforts to implement a teaching strategy that the literacy coordinator shared. The actions of followers (in this case, primarily classroom teachers) also contribute to defining leadership practice. They provide knowledge about a particular teaching strategy-knowledge that sometimes is used by leaders to illustrate a point about improving literacy instruction. (p. 145)

Essentially, distributed leadership assumes "a set of direction-setting and influence practices potentially enacted by people at all levels rather than a set of personal characteristics and attributes located in people at the top" (Leithwood, Jantzi, & McElheron-Hopkins, 2006, p. 20). Distributed leadership, then, requires interdependency and collaboration and rejects autonomy and hierarchy. Regarding the connection between distributed leadership and teacher leadership, Harris (2003) stated,

> Teacher leadership essentially refers to the exercise of leadership by teachers regardless of position or designation. In summary, teacher leadership is centrally concerned with forms of empowerment and agency, which are also at the core of distributed leadership theory . . . it is clear that there is a strong resonance between the empirical terrain provided in teacher leadership literature and the theoretical perspectives provided by those writing about distributed forms of leadership. (p. 316)

Furthermore, when Louis and Wahlstrom (2011) contacted more than 1,000 school leaders, teachers and staff, and conducted a survey of 8,000 principals and teachers to identify how schools changed and leaders operated, they concluded, "Changing a school's culture requires *shared or distributed leadership*, which engages many stakeholders in major improvement roles, and *instructional leadership*, in which administrators take responsibility for shaping improvements at the classroom level" (p. 52). This is why we believe that an understanding of the value of distributed leadership is needed for teacher leadership to flourish. That is, leadership, including teacher leadership, is not about any one person or any one situation. It is about collaboration, relationships, support, and trust as everyone works together for the good of the whole and the success of the students. As Angelle (2007) said,

> Through empowering teachers, including them in decision making, recognizing their efforts, relinquishing control, sharing responsibility for failure, and giving credit for success, principals can send the message to the school community that teacher leadership is important and accepted in the school culture. (p. 58)

Those who strive to be strong instructional leaders typically try to provide "a learning climate free of disruption, a system of clear teaching objectives, and high teacher expectations for students" (Robinson, Lloyd & Rowe, 2008, p. 638). To accomplish this, they are supportive of teacher leadership. Furthermore, the effect size, which measures the strength of the relationship between those who encourage instructional leadership and positive student outcomes was found to be a moderate .41, which was much higher than the effect size for transformational leadership, which was a weak .21 (Hattie, 2015; Robinson et al., 2008). In other words, "the mean effect size estimates for the impact of instructional leadership on student outcomes is three to four times greater than that of transformational leadership" (Robinson et al., 2008, p. 655). In sum, those focused on instructional leadership contribute to positive student outcomes, which every teacher and teacher leader also aspires to do.

Building on Hattie's (2009) research into high-impact strategies that provide visible evidence of increasing student achievement, Hattie (2015) recently stated that the High Impact Model of Instructional Leadership "isn't one in which the leader is a hero who does everything alone. Improving outcomes requires a team of teachers, students, parents, and community members, all working in collaboration" (p. 39). We argue just as Hattie (2015) wrote that "high-impact instructional leaders believe that success and failure in student learning is about what they, as teachers or leaders, did or didn't do" (p. 40); instructional leaders would say the same things about teachers as leaders.

Instructional leaders believe that the success of teachers rests on their learning, their attitude about welcoming and learning from their errors, working collaboratively, and becoming metacognitive about their teaching so that they can continue to improve. That is, instructional leaders want for teacher leaders the same goals for themselves as they have for their learners: to clearly understand what they're learning, know where they are in the learning progression, and to articulate their personal learning goals. To do this, instructional leaders create "a school climate in which everybody learns, learning is shared, and critique isn't just tolerated, but welcomed" (Hattie, 2015, p. 39). Instructional leaders do this by (a) establishing clear goals that align with positive student outcomes; (b) ensuring there are teachers and appropriate resources to support those goals; (c) actively coordinating the curriculum and evaluating the teaching in their schools, which includes being sure the progress of students is monitored; (d) actively promoting and participating in both formal and informal learning opportunities for teachers; and (e) creating a safe and supportive environment so that goals can be attained (Robinson et al., 2008). Our experience tells us that teacher leaders desire all five of these dimensions of leadership from their school leaders. However, instructional leaders know they cannot do this alone and that it requires everyone working together, which is something teacher leaders also desire and know to be both true and necessary.

SUMMARY

We believe that teacher leadership often goes unrecognized but is very important to many stakeholders in education—students, teachers, other staff, parents, and administrators. Further, we think teacher leadership should be defined first by the efforts teachers make to lead in their classrooms and then in their schools. Most teachers are already leading students in their classrooms and making use of student data discussed during professional learning community (PLC) meetings. This is, and should be, one of the first steps into teacher leadership for most teachers. Many teachers think the next step is to take on formal teacher leadership roles, but we think teacher leadership should *not* be defined only by committee assignments or promotion to grade-level or department chair. Instead, we believe that every teacher can and should take on a leadership role in some way—even new teachers. In other words, we think that teacher leadership should not be limited to formally appointed roles. Instead, teacher leadership can and should include collaborating and offering support in multiple ways to accomplish whatever is needed by students in the school for the betterment of the school as a whole. This idea was echoed by what one of our teacher leaders wrote in her journal:

> *I learned about the value of teacher leadership that it is highly important for teachers who know how to do things well within their classroom to help other teachers who ask for help. I think if this continues to happen we can strengthen the field for teachers all together. Teacher leadership is important because without it we would all stay within our classrooms, never learning about anything other teachers are doing if our students need help with topics. We need to communicate with each other, and when teachers show leadership within their school, their district, or even on a state or national level to better help the field, teachers will get more services and be more able to educate the students we teach, no matter their level.* (Tiffany, 2015)

As Tiffany noted, we agree that the second step to teacher leadership can and should include sharing what is working with other teachers in PLCs, by leading professional development sessions, and by mentoring new teachers. Teachers have expertise they have honed in their classrooms, studied in their college classes, or learned at a PD they attended, all of which they should share with others. In fact, in previous research (Levin & Schrum, 2012) we found that teachers recognized their colleagues' knowledge and preferred to learn directly from them during professional development. A third step into teacher leadership may include either regular and intermittent opportunities to tutor students, work with parents, monitor another teacher's class when asked, help the library/media specialist when students are in the media center, volunteer to attend the PTA meeting, or work with colleagues to organize a Math Night for parents. These are all forms of teacher leadership, and they all include collaborating and building relationships. Teacher leadership is also volunteering to be on a committee or starting a book club with fellow teachers, supervising preservice teachers from a local college, or arranging for snacks to celebrate Administrative Assistants' Day. Being a teacher leader may mean stepping up to help with field day or the school carnival or calling on local businesses for donations. In other words, we want to broaden the definition of teacher leadership to include all the noninstructional things teachers do, and should be acknowledged for doing, because they help others and make their school a better place for everyone. Many of these ways of leading are informal, but many teachers also take on formal leadership or hybrid roles as teacherpreneurs as well. Obviously, there are many more informal opportunities for leadership in schools than formal leadership roles, although both are important. As another of our teacher leaders said,

> *Teacher leaders are very important in changing the face of education. These individuals are at the forefront of making the necessary changes, because they have the education, experiences, courage, kind heart, and most importantly, passion . . . . Teacher leaders are needed in the school, community, and district to foster healthy educational changes.* (Bernard, 2015)

Additional activities, readings, and scenarios, and questions for reflection and discussion are available in the companion website for this book.

CHAPTER 2

What Do Teacher Leaders Need?

It is time to blur the lines of distinction between those who teach and those who lead.

(Berry, 2011)

VIEW FROM A SCHOOL LEADER	VIEW FROM A TEACHER LEADER
Mrs. Brown, I think you would make a great mentor for the beginning teachers on your team. I also think you would add an excellent perspective as a member of the school improvement committee, representing your team. Have you had any mentor training yet? If not, maybe we could look into that.	*Mr. Peterson, I really appreciate your vote of confidence, but I have not had any mentor training. I am only a third-year teacher myself, so what I know about mentoring I learned from being mentored, and that was not always the best situation. And what does the school improvement team do, exactly? I know you have regular meetings, but what would I need to do at those meetings?*

This chapter addresses ways to develop yourself as a teacher leader or promote teacher leadership in others. The first step includes understanding more about leadership styles that support teacher leadership, which we introduced in Chapter 1, and then recognizing obstacles to successful teacher leadership. This leads to some important aspects of teacher leadership, which include identifying what can be done to encourage, develop, and support teacher leaders. To address constraints on teacher leadership, we include ways to engage and reward teacher leaders based on their needs and wants. Specific questions answered in this chapter include:

1. What facilitates and nurtures teacher leadership?

2. What models of leadership, mentoring, and coaching serve teacher leaders best?

3. What hinders or stifles teacher leadership?

4. What can be done to overcome obstacles to teacher leadership?

5. What are some ways to reward teacher leaders?

WHAT FACILITATES AND NURTURES TEACHER LEADERSHIP?

Teacher leaders we have worked with told us that what helps them develop as teacher leaders and exercise teacher leadership is maintaining strong relationships with both fellow teachers and administrators. Learning about ways to collaborate with and teach other adults, and manage their time are also important factors that facilitate and nurture teacher leaders. As one of our teacher leaders reflected:

> Since teaching classrooms of children has always come pretty naturally to me, I expected that teaching adults would be just as seamless. This experience showed me that there are different challenges associated with teaching adults and that, if I am to continue my trajectory as a teacher leader, I will have to pursue professional development in this area. (Joy, 2015)

Teachers we work with do not always know what they need to be successful teacher leaders—except for "more time." However, they are able to discover both their strengths and areas they need to develop by doing self-assessments, reading, engaging in a lot of reflection, and talking with us and their peers. They also learn a lot about what inspires them to action by conducting teacher research in their classrooms and undertaking leadership projects in their schools, thus experiencing positive rewards for themselves and their colleagues. For example, Ashley (2015) captured what we also believe when she wrote,

> As a teacher leader . . . I learned that I do not have to lead alone. There are teachers willing to collaborate on a topic that they are also interested in. Making connections with other teachers is important in order to have a partner to bounce your ideas off of. We are not all experts at everything, and we need to share our knowledge with others. Part of leadership includes encouraging others to lead as well.

And Lenora (2015), a National Board Certified Teacher when we met her, wrote what she learned as a result of her teacher leadership project. Her words capture ideas we believe are important for facilitating and nurturing teacher leadership:

> Conducting this leadership project has reminded me of all the ways teachers can lead, and not just by doing professional development. Assessing the needs

of students schoolwide, collaborating with other teachers, and making an improvement plan for just one small area can make large differences in a school environment. . . . Teacher leadership is not only valuable but essential for the environment of a school, and for teachers to see themselves as career teachers—here to make a difference in the long-term.

The research literature concurs with what these teacher leaders said they learned about teacher leadership. For example, Angelle (2007) found that "[t]eachers who work in a culture of high expectations and continuous learning find that their leadership skills are actively called upon to contribute to the improvement of their school leadership abilities that might otherwise wax stagnant in other environments" (p. 57). In a study led by Crawford, Roberts, and Hickmann (2010), a three-pronged, reflective approach was developed to scaffold participants' professional growth and involvement in teacher leadership. This approach included self-study, inquiry, and action research. Early childhood educators who participated in this study gained "a greater sense of confidence, courage, collaboration, and empowerment that led to professional growth" (p. 36). This led the authors to conclude that "[t]eacher leaders, born of high-quality professional development programs, have the tacit knowledge of research-based, best practices, and possess the critical knowledge of the cultures of their home schools so necessary to facilitate change" (p. 37). While we know these things are necessary to facilitate and nurture teacher leadership, they are most often found in environments where school and district leaders espouse and enact leadership styles that support teacher leadership. Without supportive school leadership, and without effective mentoring and coaching, teacher leaders cannot flourish.

WHAT MODELS OF LEADERSHIP, MENTORING, AND COACHING SERVE TEACHER LEADERS BEST?

There are many different kinds of leadership styles used in educational settings. In Chapter 1 we proposed that transformative leadership, distributed leadership, and instructional leadership are three models supportive of teacher leadership. The main characteristics of these models of leadership are listed in Table 2.1 (Bass & Riggio, 2005; Spillane, 2005). When used actively, they can support teacher leadership.

All these leadership styles recognize the value of encouraging others to lead, given that no one person can possibly do everything needed to run a school effectively. However, Spillane (2005) does not contend that distributed leadership is "a cure-all for all that ails schools" (p. 149). Instead, he stated, "Distributed leadership is a perspective—a conceptual or diagnostic tool for thinking about school leadership. It is not a blueprint for effective leadership nor a prescription for how school leadership should be practiced" (p. 149).

TABLE 2.1 Characteristics of Transformative, Distributed, and Instructional Leadership

TRANSFORMATIVE LEADERSHIP IS ABOUT THE . . .	DISTRIBUTED LEADERSHIP IS ABOUT THE . . .	INSTRUCTIONAL LEADERSHIP IS ABOUT . . .
• Belief that leadership can occur at all levels by any individual	• Interactions among individuals vs. independence of one leader; collegiality	• Envisioning ways teachers and the school can best work together to increase student learning
• Sense of responsibility for growing and developing new leaders (known as individualized consideration)	• Shared practices and responsibilities that rest with multiple formal and informal leaders	• Believing that student learning is contingent on what teachers and leaders accomplish, or do not accomplish, together through shared leadership
• Belief that inspiring others to accomplish more than they thought possible—through support, mentoring, coaching, and serving as role models (known as idealized influence)	• Reciprocal and interdependent nature of coordinated and collaborative interactions among a network of leaders, followers, and situations	• Understanding the need for dialogue and listening to both student and teacher voices
• Development of relationships that are interdependent so people are responsible to each other	• Focus on practices of leading vs. the roles or responsibilities of individuals	• Collaborating to establish a vision and clear objectives for teaching and learning
• Empowerment of others by aligning the goals and objectives of leaders, followers, and the organization	• Routines, tools, and structures that define and/or are defined by the practices of leaders for different settings, situations, or purposes vs. fixed routines or structures	• Wanting to be an agent of change
• Motivation and involvement of others through good communication, meaningful challenges, encouragement of creative solutions, and a team spirit (known as inspirational motivation)	• Understanding that expertise is distributed across many people in a school, not just a few	• Using classroom observations and PD to focus on increasing student learning
• Respect for diversity and value of individual differences	• Understanding that distributed leadership requires a systems-thinking approach	• Using assessments to evaluate the success of everyone's efforts
		• Creating a strong academic learning culture, high expectations for students, and an environment where teachers and students view errors as learning opportunities
		• Maintaining a school environment that is conducive to learning and free of disruptions

In our experience we see that when the practices of distributed leadership are acted on, they encourage teacher leadership. Similarly, when the tenets of transformative leadership are adhered to and enacted, they are also conducive to developing the capacity for teacher leadership. The same is true in those who strive to be strong instructional leaders because they understand that everyone has to be on board and working together to achieve the goal of improving student learning and increasing student achievement, which is also a goal for every teacher and teacher leader we know. Therefore, in our view the belief in and enactment of any one of or all these styles of leadership is compatible with building the capacity for teacher leadership in schools.

To determine whether the school climate and leadership style in your workplace are supportive of teacher leadership, answer the questions in Table 2.2 to assess

TABLE 2.2   Questions for Assessing a School's Climate for Teacher Leadership

DOMAINS	QUESTIONS TO ASK ABOUT THE CLIMATE FOR TEACHER LEADERSHIP IN YOUR SCHOOL	POOR	AVERAGE	STRONG
Communication	What is your perception of the level of communication in your school from administrators to teachers?	1	2	3
	What is the level of communication among teachers and other staff members?	1	2	3
	What is the level of communication among teachers?	1	2	3
	What is the level of communication between the school and parents and families?	1	2	3
Relationships	How would you characterize the relationships between administrators and teachers?	1	2	3
	How would you characterize the relationships among the teachers and other staff?	1	2	3
	How would you characterize the relationships among the teachers?	1	2	3
	How would you characterize the relationships among the school and parents and families?	1	2	3
Collaboration	How strong is the collaboration between teachers and the administrator(s) in your school?	1	2	3
	How strong is the collaboration among teachers and other staff in your school?	1	2	3
	How strong is the collaboration among the teachers in your school?	1	2	3
	How strong is the collaboration among teachers and the parents and families in your school?	1	2	3
Knowledge	How would you characterize your administrator's level of knowledge about teacher leadership?	1	2	3
	How would you characterize the level of knowledge about teacher leadership among other staff in your school?	1	2	3
	How would you characterize the level of knowledge about teacher leadership among the teachers in your school?	1	2	3
	How would you characterize the level of knowledge about teacher leadership among your school's parents and families?	1	2	3
Support	What do you think the level of support for teacher leadership is from your administrator(s)?	1	2	3
	What do you think the level of support for teacher leadership is from other staff?	1	2	3
	What do you think the level of support for teacher leadership is from teachers?	1	2	3
	What do you think the level of support for teacher leadership is from parents and families?	1	2	3

your context. Total scores will range from 20 to 60 (and from 4–12 in each domain). Total scores of 50 to 60 indicate a strong climate and positive support for teacher leadership, while scores of 30 to 49 indicate an average climate for teacher leadership. Scores in this range should lead you to look more closely at the specific questions in domains with both stronger and weaker support for teacher leadership. Total scores below 30 indicate a poor climate for teacher leadership and the need for serious improvement in one or more domains. If you are not satisfied with the responses to any of the questions in this survey, think about and then discuss with others what teachers as leaders could do together to improve these areas.

We also realize that most teachers know intuitively, or have observed, what is and is not considered either supported or acceptable with regard to teacher leadership in their school and district. Therefore, we realize the answers to these questions are subjective and may be different depending on the day they are answered or the position and role of the person answering the questions in Table 2.2. For example, teachers new to the profession or teachers with new school leaders they do not know well may respond differently; personnel in classrooms versus those in school-wide positions such as the school librarian or media specialist, assistant principal, or school counselor or psychologist might also have a different perspective. Therefore, we think it would be very useful to ask as many teachers and other staff members as possible, and also parents and administrators, to respond to these questions. The more data you can gather, the more likely the results will be representative of the school's climate and support for teacher leadership. In addition, asking others may lead to some good discussions about ways to improve the climate for teacher leadership. Answers to these questions may reveal a need for overall improvement, or they might reveal a need for improvement in only a few domains. Identified areas for improvement can be a focus for the actions and advocacy by teacher leaders (see more about advocacy in Chapter 7). Teacher leaders we have worked with who reflected on their school's climate for teacher leadership found clear areas for growth, as this reflection describes.

> The [collaboration] score did not surprise me at all because we are a small staff; some departments only have one member. There have not been many opportunities for people to share best practices, and some colleagues do not show any interest in working with others. I think this hurts our school climate and needs great improvement . . . . The communication score was very accurate because for the last two of the three years . . . . we have constantly expressed our concern that we never know what is going on, or when we are told, the plan is never clear. I think this is the most frustrating because we want to be informed and are not. I am hoping this will change soon . . . I am not surprised by the results, but I am saddened and frustrated because I think my school has the potential to be an amazing school; however, we are not doing things to the best of our ability. (Cappy, 2014)

There are other surveys we recommend regarding a school's readiness for teacher leadership (see Katzenmeyer & Moller, 2009), and there are also online surveys that can be very useful for considering additional aspects related to what schools and school leaders could be doing to support teacher leadership. One survey for assessing school culture, which has strong reliability, can be found in Appendix A, and there is another survey for assessing a school's readiness to change its culture that can be found in Appendix C.

ACTIVITY: There are three surveys available online from the Center for Strengthening the Teaching Profession (CSTP). The links are provided on our companion website. These include a comprehensive Teacher Leadership Skills Framework, a Teacher Leader Skills Assessment, and a School and District Capacity Tool. We recommend using each of these tools for further self-assessment of both one's individual skills related to teacher leadership and to further assess the climate and readiness of a school or district for supporting teacher leadership. After completing these surveys, a rich discussion should ensue from the results. Comparing the probable differences among individuals' answers will highlight the importance of school context when considering readiness for teacher leadership.

Mentoring and Coaching to Support Teacher Leadership. In addition to evaluating the climate for supporting teacher leadership, it is important to consider models for mentoring and coaching that serve teacher leaders. This information can help teacher leaders advocate for the kinds of support they need. We know from personal experience and research on mentoring beginning teachers, mentors, and support providers that teacher leaders need ongoing mentoring and support themselves (McQuillin, Straight, & Saeki, 2015; see also the New Teacher Center at www.newteachercenter.org/mentors). Even though people act as teacher leaders, they do not automatically know everything needed to be as successful a leader as possible. In fact, without support and mentoring, we have seen teacher leaders burn out or drop out. Therefore, we recommend these steps:

- First, school and/or district leaders must make the expectations they have for teacher leaders explicit and clear to them and to the rest of the staff. If they do not, then teacher leaders must ask for clear directions so they understand what is expected of them.

- Second, to ensure their success, professional development (PD) for and mentoring or coaching of teacher leaders is necessary. However, because effective mentoring includes sharing one's thinking and decision making, clear expectations should be the first thing a school leader offers teacher leaders.

- Third, it is naïve to assume that every teacher leader knows what to do and has the skills to accomplish the task(s) asked of them; lacking certain skills may be a recipe for failure. School leaders who espouse and enact transformative and/or distributed leadership know this, but it is important for teacher leaders to know themselves well enough to ask for modeling, mentoring, or coaching.

- Fourth, teacher leaders should set their own very clear personal and professional goals for their leadership project or leadership responsibilities based on the expectations set for them. To be most effective, these goals should be written, discussed, and signed off by both teacher leaders and those responsible for supporting or evaluating them. Most likely this will be an administrator or another school leader, but having a kind of "contract" is one way to support teacher leaders.

- Fifth, we think it is crucial for teacher leaders to enlist others to collaborate with them rather than try to take on any task or responsibility alone. It does no good to try doing everything alone and become a martyr, because that will discourage future teacher leadership. Building a team will assist teacher leaders while simultaneously creating teacher support for desired goals.

- Sixth, teacher leaders should seek ongoing support and feedback as needed from their school leader(s) or other mentors. To do this all parties should engage in regular, two-way, transparent communication so that any issues can be discussed and resolved. Good communication must include all parties involved.

- Seventh, if problems arise, teacher leaders may need to ask for more support from others or make use of conflict resolution skills. Good communication and other skills needed by all teacher leaders are discussed further in Chapters 4 and 5.

One mentoring model for supporting teacher leaders is the formation of coaching partnerships among experienced and novice teacher leaders, or between two or three teacher leaders, whether they are experienced or not. Alternatively, an experienced school or teacher leader could be asked to coach a small group of teacher leaders. We saw an example of teacher leaders supporting each other during a recent teacher leadership course when a developing teacher leader took the initiative to meet with other teacher leaders in her school to create a support group. This developing teacher leader focused her teacher research project and her teacher leadership project around supporting the mentor teachers in her school. As a mentor of new teachers herself, she felt she needed more support than she was getting. Even though she had received some professional development about mentoring new teachers in previous years, she and other mentors at her school had not received any support since their initial training. Here is how Stephanie (2015) described her efforts:

Mentors are often identified based on their successful work with students; however, many lack the necessary skills and knowledge to adequately support novice teachers. Therefore, it is imperative that mentors receive adequate and ongoing professional development as they support and guide beginning teachers. As a mentor myself, this issue is very important to me because I understand first-hand the struggle to help novice teachers with little to no support of my own. . . . As I conducted research for my Teacher Research project, I discovered a large amount of data that spoke to the importance of, and necessity for, professional development for mentors. The studies I encountered supported the findings from my initial Teacher Research surveys, as well as my discussions with the collaborators and participants in this study, regarding the overall lack of continued support and training for mentors. While I felt that this was an issue personally, I was surprised to realize that fellow colleagues, as well as teacher researchers around the country, shared this concern. . . . Our conversation opened our eyes to the fact that we can be the support system for one another's needs as we face the challenging task of effectively mentoring our novice teachers. . . . My Teacher Research project uncovered a need at my specific school, and through this Leadership project, I was able to advocate for a change in practice that would fill this need. . . . It is my hope that I have laid the foundation for a Mentor Team that will continue to meet and support one another, while also seeking out and providing development opportunities that will further their abilities as mentors.

The New Teacher Center (NTC; www.newteachercenter.org) also recommends "mentor shadowing" as a model for developing and supporting mentor teachers (Cox, 2007, p. 8). We think this model would work well for mentoring teacher leaders as well. For starters it would mean asking prospective teacher leaders to first shadow and then colead with another teacher leader. In fact, we think coleading is an ideal situation because as we have stated before, no one should try to lead alone. Furthermore, shadowing provides support for both new and experienced teacher leaders, and new teacher leaders are better prepared to take on new roles when more experienced teacher leaders are ready to move on. These strategies work well for both formal and informal teacher leadership roles and responsibilities and serve as a good way to induct newer teachers into leadership positions. In addition, the NTC found reciprocal benefits for both the experienced and novice teacher leaders when shadowing a mentor. Mentor shadowing also clarifies the expectations for leadership and allows new teacher leaders to determine if particular teacher leadership responsibilities match their talents, interests, and strengths.

The NTC also recommends online mentoring support, although we think this might be less conducive to coaching teacher leaders because it may not account for the local context and school culture. However, for some teacher leaders, participating in an online forum can offer needed support for those who have dilemmas they feel they cannot reveal to others in their school. Participating in an online forum can also provide a variety of opinions about how a teacher leader might handle something tricky at their location. The Center for Teaching Quality (http://www.teachingquality.org/) is one of several online places teacher leaders can go to for support, problem solving, new ideas, and even professional development.

Teacher leaders should also consider establishing their own online Personal Learning Networks (PLNs) as a model for both support and for continued learning. Participating with other educators in an online environment can be used very effectively for professional learning about the knowledge and skills needed by teacher leaders. This can happen via Twitter, by participating on online forums, or simply by reading blogs written by other teacher leaders. Finally, sending teacher leaders to state, regional, or national conferences where they can network with, learn from, and develop as teacher leaders is another model for supporting and mentoring teacher leaders.

WHAT HINDERS OR STIFLES TEACHER LEADERSHIP?

Unfortunately, there are many things that keep teachers from being leaders. These include the fact that teachers are typically overworked and underpaid, their time for additional duties is finite, the accountability system discourages rather than rewards teacher leadership-type activities, and there is often a lack of support from other teachers (Angelle, 2007; Barth, 2001; Katzenmeyer & Moller, 2009). These issues often give teachers pause when they consider taking on teacher leadership responsibilities. A perceived lack of leadership skills can also place constraints on teacher leadership (Katzenmeyer & Moller, 2009).

Among the impediments to teacher leadership, the most disappointing to us is the "tall poppy syndrome" or the "crab bucket" mentality described by Katzenmeyer and Moller (2009). This happens when teachers, who may not want others to lead or stand out, engage in active or passive efforts to "pull down" teacher leaders. In many places the egalitarian nature of the teaching profession is a detriment to teacher leadership, and the culture is such that teachers are afraid to step up as leaders because they fear losing the support of their friends or being accused of siding with administration. Capturing the concerns of the many teacher leaders we have worked with, Allison (2014) expressed not only a concern they all felt, but also what can be done to overcome this obstacle to teacher leadership.

> *I think this is the hardest obstacle to navigate as a teacher leader. Because teaching is a flat profession, leadership roles are often seen as threatening to other teachers. Again, communication is very important with peers—teacher leaders must have good conflict resolution skills and listening skills. They must be seen as a benefit to fellow teachers instead of a threat. Developing*

strong, caring relationships with colleagues will go a long way in building trust. In this way, teachers will feel more open to receiving feedback (both positive and negative) from teacher leaders.

School leaders who do not make teacher leadership available for everyone, or who show favoritism, may unwittingly compound the lack of support by teachers for others who become teacher leaders. As discussed earlier, this dilemma is further confounded when school leaders, for example, are not transparent or clear regarding what they expect of a teacher leader, or why they selected one teacher over another. However, as Angelle (2007) noted, "[u]nfortunately, the greatest resistance to teacher leadership may come from colleagues. Fellow teachers do not always embrace their colleagues as leaders" (p. 59). Therefore, to ensure success for teacher leaders, school culture must value their efforts, school leaders must support their work, and teacher colleagues must be willing to work alongside them as they strive to make their workplace more effective. Another hindrance to teacher leadership is that

> Most teachers who take on leadership roles do not see themselves as leaders, reserving the term leader for those who take on formal roles, such as principals or district supervisors. Instead, they perceive that most of their work is done informally through collaboration. (Moller, Childs-Bowen, & Scrivner, 2001, as cited in Angelle, 2007, p. 54)

Therefore, teachers need their school and district leaders to create a culture that supports, recognizes, and rewards teacher leadership. They also need PD to help them grow and develop as teacher leaders, which is what this book is all about. Just asking teachers to lead without supporting them is likely to result in individual failures that could be avoided. Teacher leadership, then, is the responsibility of not just teachers who want to be teacher leaders, but of all school and district leaders, and other teachers as well.

ACTIVITY: Use role playing as a strategy for problem solving. First, think through how you would answer the questions posed in this activity. Then with a partner or in a small group, use these questions to role play conversations among fellow teachers and/or with your school leaders. (1) As a beginning teacher, how should I ask my school leader for support? (2) As a novice teacher leader, how should I suggest something that needs improving or fixing in the school? (3) How could my school leader demonstrate his or her support for an initiative I propose as a teacher leader? (4) How should I talk with colleagues who have not embraced my new role as a teacher leader? (5) How might I enlist support from other teachers so I do not have to go it alone?

WHAT CAN BE DONE TO OVERCOME OBSTACLES TO TEACHER LEADERSHIP?

We think a teacher leader we taught recently captured the answer to this question quite profoundly when she expressed her understanding that good communication, relationships, support, and trust are keys to overcoming obstacles to teacher leadership.

> *One way that teacher leaders can overcome obstacles is by arranging support at the school or district level. Colleagues can see a teacher leader as a threat to them, so if teacher leaders are supported by their administrators and fellow teachers, they will be more effective in their work. In addition, both trust and communication are key for teacher leaders to overcome obstacles. There needs to be open communication and a trusting relationship between administrators, teacher leaders, and teachers at a school.* (Holly, 2014)

We know that school and district leaders play important roles by supporting teacher leadership (Collinson & Cook, 2004; Katzenmeyer & Moller, 2009; Raffanti, 2008). They can create a culture of embracing teacher leadership in their schools and districts in many ways, although in all cases good communication, relationships, support, and trust are key. As described earlier, the first suggestion we make is for administrators to enact the tenets of distributed, transformative, and instructional leadership (see Table 2.1) in their daily practice and through their policies and hiring practices. The second is to actively and publicly promote teacher leadership at every opportunity by educating staff, school board members, parents and families, and the wider school community about the value added when teachers serve as leaders in their schools. Katzenmeyer and Moller (2009) stated that teacher leaders must be disposed to take risks, be persistent, challenge existing practices, feel a sense of efficacy, and be resilient. To accomplish these things, school and district leaders need to find ways to support and reward teacher leaders, and to encourage and recognize the activities of those teachers.

> Through empowering teachers, including them in decision making, recognizing their efforts, relinquishing control, sharing responsibility for failure, and giving credit for success, principals can send the message to the school community that teacher leadership is important and accepted in the school culture. (Angelle, 2007, p. 58)

Another obstacle to making teacher leadership ubiquitous is the need for professional development. According to the research literature, ongoing, high-quality PD is key for developing and sustaining teacher leaders (Copeland & Gray, 2002; Crawford et al., 2010), but this rarely happens. Instead teachers are asked to take on leadership roles, whether formally or informally, without adequate preparation. Teachers usually know their own strengths and weaknesses, but not always. They know they need to learn ways to lead and desire to have the needed knowledge and skills for teacher leadership. Therefore, it benefits school and district leaders to not only explicitly name the strengths they see in teachers they ask to lead, but also provide support and training in areas that will help teacher leaders be more successful. This is equally true for already experienced teacher leaders and potential future teacher leaders.

One simple way to begin recognizing and developing teacher leaders is to ask teachers to share their strengths and accomplishments during faculty meetings. The sharing of teacher expertise and successful classroom practices creates a positive culture of appreciation for the efforts teachers make in their classrooms. When recognition becomes a regular part of meetings, and different teachers are asked to share each time, the climate of the school improves (Levin & Schrum, 2012). This is also compatible with the notions of transformative, distributed, and instructional leadership, which we see as leadership styles that foster teacher leadership. These meetings could also be a time to celebrate risk taking and making it safe to try things and learn from mistakes, which is a key feature of instructional leadership (Hattie, 2015).

Another simple way to develop a climate for teacher leadership is to create a culture in the school that expects everyone to contribute in some way and then recognizes everyone's contribution. This doesn't necessarily mean everyone has to be on a committee, but that everyone agrees to do something positive for the students and the school every semester. Given that having choice is a big motivator, giving teachers a choice in how they demonstrate leadership seems logical, empowering, and a better strategy than assigning people to tasks they may not be suited for or want to do.

Finally, another way to overcome obstacles to teacher leadership is to share and discuss the Model Teacher Leader Standards found in Chapter 1. These standards provide a good starting point for discussing what teacher leadership could look like in any school. They can be used to engage teachers in discussing what results teacher leadership might produce as a core value in a school. These standards are also a good starting point for talking about the many possible responsibilities of teacher leaders in particular school contexts. The Model Teacher Leadership Standards can also be used as a starting point for brainstorming ways teachers could engage in leadership (see Table 1.2 for examples).

WHAT ARE SOME WAYS TO REWARD TEACHER LEADERS?

While most teachers do what they do without expecting to be recognized or rewarded, because that's who teachers are, this does not mean that they should not be recognized or rewarded in some way. This could include tangible rewards, but many teachers may also value intangible rewards. The best advice is for leaders to ask.

When we asked a group of teacher leaders to brainstorm intangible, no-cost ways they would like to be rewarded for their efforts, their ideas were both simple and profound. As can be seen in Table 2.3, their collective suggestions represent how little it takes for most teacher leaders to continue working hard for their students, their schools, and their profession. However, teacher leaders are not all motivated by the same things, so it is important to learn what each teacher views as a positive reward for their efforts. It may be as simple as verbal recognition, which costs nothing, but differentiating how teacher leaders are encouraged and rewarded is worth the time to figure out.

TABLE 2.3   Ways to Reward Teacher Leaders

Verbal affirmation—Staff members, and especially administrators, could offer verbal feedback to teacher leaders, thanking and praising them for specific accomplishments. This could be a private conversation, an e-mail, or even a hand-written note. A nice pat on the back goes a long way!

Recognition in front of peers—This could be tricky because you don't want to create a competitive environment. But if teacher leaders are going above and beyond, they could be recognized at a staff meeting, on the morning show, in a staff e-mail or weekly update, and on the school's website. In one school we know of, they dedicate the first 5 minutes of each staff meeting to recognizing faculty who go above and beyond.

Peer-to-peer recognition—Leave sticky notes or postcards in the teachers' lounge and/or workroom so peers can leave thank you notes or praise for each other.

Comp time—If teacher leaders work beyond their normal working hours, they should receive comp time to be used on workdays or snow days. Typically, teacher leaders are the first ones in the building and the last ones out. By allowing teacher leaders to log this time and then use it on non-mandated workdays, such as snow days or at the end of the year, they will see that their work and time are appreciated.

Dress-down day—Permission to wear jeans or dress down on casual Fridays.

Acceptance of ideas—This is a great idea because it values the teacher and costs nothing. For instance, I suggested the book club idea for my teacher leadership project and my principal absolutely loved the idea. This also allows teacher leaders to rise up within the school community.

Create a school bulletin board that highlights teacher leader contributions in the workroom or teachers' lounge, and/or recognize a "teacher leader of the week" in school announcements.

Duty-free periods, or trading out planning time—We could ALL use extra planning time. Having someone sit in on your class for 30 minutes and take over while you can step away for a bit would be great—so would being relieved from one of our duties or somehow compensated for the extra time we put in by being excused from something else. A member of the administrative team could cover one of the duties once in a while!

Duty-free lunch—A duty pass/duty-free lunch would be a tangible reward!

Greater decision-making power—Being asked for input, to vote on ideas being considered, or even doing a survey or needs assessment before decisions are made would feel empowering. Opportunities to participate (with teams and/or administration) and contribute to decision making is very rewarding for teachers.

First consideration when special opportunities come up—Being invited to present to the faculty and staff, attend a PD, go to a conference, and so on is highly valued.

Ask the Parent-Teacher Organization to come up with some type of reward (lunch, breakfast, or snacks through donations) to acknowledge teacher leaders.

Get businesses in the community to donate gift cards, services, or some small gift to reward teachers' efforts.

Schedule longer lunches on teacher workdays—This would be a simple way to thank every teacher, but it is an especially great way to recognize teacher leaders who go above and beyond. Going off-campus for lunch is a real treat!

Include time to share new ideas or strategies at staff/faculty functions.

Encouragement and opportunities to implement new strategies nurture the professionalism of teachers who want to continue to grow and develop.

Recruit students who need community service hours to help the teacher leaders. These students may clean their classroom, file papers, organize materials, and so on.

Personal days or work-at-home days—Might be possible for teacher leaders without classroom duties.

Special parking spaces—In some schools, this would really be appreciated.

Simply by treating teacher leaders like professional human beings who deserve respect.

ACTIVITY: Generate your own list of rewards you think teacher leaders deserve. Include both tangible and intangible rewards. Then think realistically about what rewards would be viable in your workplace and brainstorm ways to make those rewards happen. Alternatively, prioritize the ideas in Table 2.3 to indicate what would be most rewarding for you.

While most teachers and teacher leaders are happy to be recognized and rewarded with intangibles, we believe teacher leaders should be compensated financially in addition to being acknowledged publicly. In fact, Harris (2003) claimed:

> While it could be argued that teacher leadership brings its own reward, through enhanced effectiveness, a sense of collegiality, improved teaching practices, etc., it will remain a marginal activity within schools unless forms of remuneration are put in place to actively encourage teachers to engage in leadership tasks. (p. 320)

How this happens in tight budget times is tricky. Fortunately, Margolis and Deuel (2009) found that teacher leaders were motivated by both intrinsic rewards (related to their educational moral beliefs of what is right and wrong) and extrinsic rewards (like money). They also found that the teacher leadership title meant little to the teacher leaders. And most important, they found that teacher leaders have significant capacity to effect instructional change.

Nevertheless, public recognition, release time, new job titles, career ladders, additional education, and commensurate compensation are all needed if we want to keep many of our teacher leaders. Of all these, time and recognition are the most realistic and the most appreciated by most teacher leaders (Schrum & Levin, 2015). However, in places where there is a career path for teacher leaders, we know that many are interested in taking on the roles of coaching other teachers and facilitating teacher learning in their schools. Nevertheless, because we value what both formal and informal teacher leaders contribute, we hope everyone who reads this book will thank a teacher to encourage more teacher leadership!

ACTIVITY: Think about other teachers, teacher leaders, and school leaders whose efforts you appreciate. Then write a thank you note or a thank you e-mail to that person. As part of your thank you, explicitly acknowledge the value their leadership efforts have added to your workplace and encourage them to continue being a role model for others.

SUMMARY

In this chapter we discussed what facilitates and nurtures teacher leadership, including, but not limited to: the gift of time, trusted colleagues willing to work collaboratively, and the guidance of school leaders who understand how to support their teacher leaders. We believe that teacher leadership cannot flourish without supportive school leadership, or without effective mentoring and coaching for both new and experienced teacher leaders. We also described features of transformative, distributed, and instructional leadership, which are three leadership styles supportive of teacher leadership. In addition, we discussed the importance of a school's readiness for teacher leadership and provided a survey instrument to assess whether your school is supportive of teacher leadership in the areas of communication, relations, collaboration, knowledge, and support. We suggested that this survey, and others with similar goals, should be used to identify strengths and weaknesses so that actions can be taken to improve weaker areas and celebrate and nurture stronger areas.

We also discussed specific steps and strategies for mentoring and coaching teacher leaders including coaching partnerships, shadowing other leaders, and opportunities for coleadership. These strategies and additional PD about the knowledge and skills needed for teacher leadership are key to developing a supportive culture for teacher leadership. Without such supports, teacher leadership will be stifled because we already ask so much of teachers without always acknowledging or rewarding them for their extra efforts. Good communication, positive relationships, support, and trust are keys to overcoming obstacles to teacher leadership. However, while we believe these things are all necessary, they are not sufficient. While many teachers are willing to go above and beyond to lead both inside and beyond their classrooms, we also described many ways to reward and compensate teacher leaders—not the least of which is monetary compensation for their leadership efforts.

In sum, we know that when teachers are prepared for leadership roles, they will be more likely to step up and they will be more successful, which benefits everyone. We also know that school leaders can find ways to purposefully develop their teacher leaders. This can be done by apprenticing them to already experienced teacher leaders, by coaching and mentoring them, and by using this book as a resource for PD sessions, in PLCs, or through a book study. Additional activities, readings, and scenarios and questions for reflection and discussion are available in the companion website for this book.

CHAPTER 3

Dispositions for Teacher Leadership

It is not enough to be compassionate. You must act.

—Dalai Lama

VIEW FROM A SCHOOL LEADER	VIEW FROM A TEACHER LEADER
Mrs. Brown, I really think you have the right dispositions to be a strong teacher leader. You are a very positive and caring teacher, and I know you are hardworking. I think other teachers respect your ideas and would listen to you. You will learn a lot from collaborating with other teacher leaders about what works on the school improvement team, but I am also willing to help you set some specific goals.	*Mr. Peterson, one of my goals is to get my master's degree, so I wonder if I can handle being a mentor and on the school improvement team and do a good job in my master's course. I know I am a hard worker, but I also know that my colleagues still see me as a novice teacher. I wonder if they will listen to my ideas or think someone with more experience should be a teacher leader in our school.*

It is highly likely that you, and others you work with, have ideas about who teacher leaders are and how they should act, including what their temperament, nature, character, personal qualities, or habits of mind should be. "Dispositions" is the term we use in this chapter to describe the mind-set and conduct expected of teacher leaders. Dispositions are the source of one's thoughts, attitudes, feelings, and beliefs; they also guide one's actions. This is why dispositions must be considered along with the knowledge and skills needed by teacher leaders. Therefore, in this chapter we focus on dispositions needed for teacher leadership. We discuss ways teacher leaders can establish a vision and goals for teacher leadership that are reflective of their dispositions. We also offer a method for assessing your dispositional readiness and self-efficacy for teacher leadership. To accomplish these goals, we include several activities, scenarios for discussion, and additional resources in the online companion guide for this book that are designed to help teacher leaders consciously consider who they want to be as teacher leaders.

In our experience, considering dispositions needed for successful teacher leadership serves as a catalyst for developing awareness about what it takes to be a teacher leader. With this in mind, we have been asking teacher leaders to think about, write about, and discuss the questions listed below for several years. We have provided opportunities for self-assessment and reflection about dispositions to help teacher leaders begin thinking metacognitively about teacher leadership. Specific questions we address in this chapter include:

1. What dispositions do others expect from you and other teacher leaders?

2. What have you accomplished so far as a teacher leader?

3. What is your vision for teacher leadership?

4. What are your goals for teacher leadership in the next 1, 5, and 10 years?

5. What image or metaphor would you choose for yourself as a teacher leader?

6. What obstacles do you need to overcome to become a strong teacher leader?

7. How can you overcome obstacles to teacher leadership?

WHAT DISPOSITIONS DO OTHERS EXPECT FROM YOU AND OTHER TEACHER LEADERS?

We have specific expectations about dispositions of teachers; for example, we expect teachers to hold the belief that all children can learn. Dispositions are often used to describe both how teacher leaders should behave and what they should believe. Along with knowledge and skills, dispositions are used to talk about what others expect of teachers who are leaders. In Chapter 1, we included a list of dispositions culled from what others have written to describe teacher leaders: flexible, open, caring, driven, supportive, determined, cheerful, consistent, positive, approachable, active, patient, persistent, tactful, self-efficacious, and ethical (see Table 1.1). The 2013 Council for the Accreditation of Educator Preparation Programs (CAEP) standards describe dispositions as mind-sets that include "coachability, empathy, teacher presence of 'with-it-ness,' cultural competency, collaboration, beliefs, that all children can learn" (p. 49). Critical dispositions are described by the Interstate Teacher Assessment and Support Consortium (InTASC) Model Core Teaching Standards as "habits of professional action and moral commitments that underlie the performances [and] play a key role in how teachers do, in fact, act in practice" (CCSSO, 2011, p. 6). They include "problem solving, curiosity, creativity, innovation, communication, interpersonal skills, the ability to synthesize across disciplines, global awareness, ethics, and technological expertise" (CCSSO, 2011, p. 4).

All teachers communicate a set of expectations and encourage particular dispositions in their classrooms, whether they do this consciously or not. However, we know that teachers in leadership positions are not always told explicitly what is expected of them, therefore dispositions expected of teacher leaders often have to be inferred. We think there are some universal dispositions that should be expected of all teacher leaders, which include caring, fairness, honesty, responsibility, and commitment to social justice. We also understand that different dispositions may be emphasized in different contexts. However, we believe that dispositions needed by teacher leaders are not finite or fixed, and there is no one correct set of dispositions for teacher leadership. We also believe that dispositions can be developed and nurtured, especially in contexts where they are articulated clearly as a set of aspirational values or as part of the culture of a school. Therefore, we think that teacher leaders, and school leaders as well, should be explicit about the dispositions they believe are important, strive to enact them, and seek to cultivate them in others.

The dispositions listed in Table 3.1 include what the teachers we have worked with in the past said are important for teacher leadership. They are listed in no particular order, but we offer them here so that teacher leaders might consider which of these are among their strengths and/or might become aspirations as they grow and develop as teacher leaders.

> *Teacher leaders, and school leaders as well, should be explicit about the dispositions they believe are important, strive to enact them, and seek to cultivate them in others.*

To discuss dispositions, it is important to create a safe, judgment-free, and positive atmosphere for talking about dispositions. It is also important to provide background information, and create experiences for teacher leaders to explore and discover ways to understand not only dispositions needed by teacher leaders, but also ways to personally reveal, develop, and carry out desired dispositions. Several ways to accomplish this are described in the remainder of this chapter and in the online companion guide for this book.

TABLE 3.1   Dispositions for Teacher Leadership

DISPOSITIONS TEACHERS SAY ARE NEEDED FOR LEADERSHIP			
• Open-minded	• Optimistic	• Patient	• Passionate
• Humble	• Persuasive	• Brave	• Invested
• Respectful	• Enthusiastic	• Adaptable	• Focused
• Flexible	• Risk taker	• Positive	• Great communicator
• Collegial	• Confident	• Reliable	• Act on intuition—what is best for the kids
• Energetic	• Decisive	• Flexible	• Prepared
• Creative	• Tolerant of ambiguity	• Good listener	• Respectful
• Persistent	• Hardworking	• Self-confident	• Willing to compromise
• Engaged	• Ethical	• Self-motivated	
• Resourceful	• Accepting	• Organized	
• Courageous		• Lifelong learner	

WHAT HAVE YOU ACCOMPLISHED
SO FAR AS A TEACHER LEADER?

The first step in considering dispositions needed for teacher leadership is to determine what teacher leadership includes and ways teachers demonstrate leadership. According to Katzenmeyer and Moller (2009), teacher leadership is often demonstrated in one of three ways: through teaching and learning, by influencing school-wide policies and programs, or through communications and community relations. In addition, based on the Teacher Leadership Model Standards found in Table 1.3, teacher leaders demonstrate leadership when they advocate for students, mentor new teachers, inform others by sharing their knowledge, connect with the community, connect with parents and families, teach others, communicate by being a voice for the profession and sharing their experiences, and collaborate with others. With all these in mind regarding what teacher leaders do, we begin a conversation about dispositions for teacher leadership by first asking the teachers we work with about the ways they are already leading or have led in the past. In our experience, teachers typically understand and will claim the formal leadership roles they have been appointed to or elected to fulfill, such as being grade-level or department chair. However, they often need examples of informal leadership roles, which include sharing new or successful practices with others, helping new teachers, volunteering to serve on a committee, writing grants to support classroom or school activities, helping others solve technology issues, and so on.

ACTIVITY: Using the informal and formal leadership roles and responsibilities you have had in and out of school in the past and now, organize them into these three categories: instructional, organizational, and professional. Refer to Tables 1.2 and 3.2 to help you see all the ways other teachers lead both formally and informally inside and outside school. You may see some things you have done, or are doing now, that are examples of teacher leadership you did not initially recognize. If so, add them to your list and then look to see where your strengths and interests as a teacher leader are manifested now. Use this information to help you set a goal for future teacher leadership.

We always write everything they have accomplished collectively on a whiteboard, poster paper, or in a Google Doc to display the depth and breadth of what teachers do to demonstrate leadership. The list of leadership opportunities that are revealed is always astonishing, both to us and to all the teachers in the room, because teachers do not typically give themselves credit for all the ways they show leadership. Often they tell us what they do is just part of their job, or part of their life outside school. We, however, want them to recognize that they are already demonstrating leadership in many ways. This leads us to several activities related to how they want to be as teacher leaders going forward, what dispositions they

TABLE 3.2   Examples of Teachers Leading Inside and Outside School

FORMAL TEACHER LEADERSHIP IN SCHOOL	INFORMAL TEACHER LEADERSHIP IN SCHOOL	TEACHERS LEADING OUTSIDE OF SCHOOL
• Serving on the school improvement committee or leadership team • Creating schoolwide policies for student conduct, attendance, grading, homework, etc. • Initiating and leading cocurricular activities • Mentoring and coaching new teachers • Assisting in hiring new staff • Organizing a cross-age tutoring program • Leading professional development activities by either making a presentation or sharing a successful practice or strategy • Overseeing the school website • Developing a schoolwide process to monitor student progress from grade to grade	• Arranging social programs for faculty and staff • Instituting student-led parent conferences • Experimenting with flipped instruction • Encouraging student and/or teacher volunteer service activities • Providing families with information about how to support student learning • Initiating a family reading program in the school library • Communicating positive information to parents • Organizing a parent/family night to explain a new curriculum • Organizing a parent/family information session about student developmental issues	• Scout leader or coleader • Sunday school leader—develop curriculum, and organize volunteer teachers • Neighborhood watch chair • Leadership position and/or committee chair in civic organizations • Religious leader and other leadership positions at religious institution • Heading up a fund-raising event for a health organization • Organizing a silent auction as a fund-raiser • Coaching a sports team

want to display, how they want others to describe them, what their vision is for themselves as teacher leaders, and what their specific goals are.

Teachers do not typically give themselves credit for all the ways they show leadership.

Once we have a good understanding about all the ways teachers are already leading, we ask teacher leaders what they think it takes to be a teacher leader. Typically, we ask them what knowledge, skills, and dispositions they think teacher leaders need. When they think about and generate lists about what is knowledge versus what is a skill versus what is a disposition, the distinctions are not always clear. However, this is not as important as reflecting on what they think teacher leaders need to know and be able to do well, and what dispositions they should be striving to enact as teacher leaders. Nevertheless, we do ask them to reflect on and write about what knowledge and skills they feel they already have, and what dispositions they feel are already strengths. Then we use their input to help us plan what needs to be practiced or reinforced and what they still need to learn. The knowledge and skills we have found they need to learn are the focus of the next four chapters in this book, so we do not address them here. Instead, we continue to focus on dispositions for teacher leadership in the remainder of this chapter.

ACTIVITY: To reflect again on what you are learning and thinking about teacher leadership, choose one of these options and respond to the questions posed:

Option 1. What knowledge, skills, and dispositions do you think teacher leaders need to possess? Either make three lists or write three sentences that list the dispositions, knowledge, and skills needed for effective teacher leadership. Mark with a star or asterisk what you most want to learn related to being an effective teacher leader.

Option 2. Make a T-chart and list your strengths in one column and areas for growth in the other column with regard to the dispositions, knowledge, and skills needed for teacher leadership. Be sure to give yourself credit for what you already know and can do as a teacher leader, but also think about what you still want to learn and hope to accomplish.

WHAT IS YOUR VISION FOR TEACHER LEADERSHIP?

The next step related to dispositions for teacher leadership is to think about what you would most like to accomplish as a teacher leader. In other words, what is your vision for yourself as a teacher leader? Visioning about teacher leadership is the process of reflecting on one's sense of self as a teacher who leads and one's personal ambitions and goals for how to be as a leader. We believe that visioning is a crucial process for teacher leaders to engage in because a vision can serve as a moral or cognitive compass that can be used to guide one's practice (Cooper, He, & Levin, 2011). In fact, Shulman (2004) suggested that visioning may be the "missing construct" in identifying high-quality teachers, and Hammerness and her colleagues (2005) consider visioning to be a process that teachers can use to develop their professional identity. The end goal of visioning is a statement about what kind of teacher leader you want to be and how you want others to see you as a leader. In the process of creating a vision, your dispositions are revealed, or at least implied.

A vision for teacher leadership, then, serves as a personal commitment to become the kind of leader you aspire to be. Some visions for teacher leadership focus on either a moral or an intellectual outcome that guides interactions with others. However, visions also express personal self-understandings, so they are helpful in developing metacognitive thinking about teacher leadership, which we think is an important type of knowledge to cultivate in teacher leaders.

There are several ways to elicit visions for teacher leadership. Next, we share the activity we use most often, although it is simple enough to just ask teachers what vision they have for themselves as teacher leaders, what they most want to accomplish, and how they want others to see them as a teacher leader. At the end of our time together, we usually return to the first vision statement that teacher leaders developed and ask them to revise their vision based on what they have learned and experienced regarding teacher leadership. As a result, we often see a shift in their vision, which shows growth in becoming a teacher leader.

ACTIVITY: Use this four-step process to create your vision for teacher leadership. Write your answers to each question after taking some time to think about them.

1. Think about why you chose to become an educator in the first place. Reflect on your personal values and prior leadership experiences, including both in-school experiences and out-of-school experiences. What personal strengths make you a good teacher and a good leader? Describe the values, skills, strengths, and qualities you bring to your classroom and your school.

2. Imagine 5 to 10 years from now when you see the people you work with again. What would they say to you? What would you say when you are interviewed as a recipient of the Excellence Award for Teacher Leadership? What does a person with your values, skills, strengths, and qualities want to accomplish next? What do you hope and dream to achieve? What would the ideal environment for successful teacher leadership look like for you?

3. What will you do to achieve your dreams as a teacher leader? Which of your strengths, skills, and qualities will you use to attain your vision?

4. What knowledge or experiences do you think you need to have to achieve your dream? What actions do you plan on taking to become an excellent teacher leader? What are the first steps? What might be your obstacles? What would you do if you face those challenges?

As mentioned above, we ask teachers these three questions to elicit their visions: What is your vision for yourself as a teacher leader? What do you feel you would most like to accomplish as a teacher leader? How do you want others to describe you as a teacher leader? Here are some statements about the visions of teacher leaders we know:

As a teacher leader, I would want others to describe me as innovative, hard-working, and someone who thinks outside of the box. I enjoy filling niches where there is a need and I generally am the one who likes to fix problems and create peace. I do not do well in circumstances of conflict, so I would be the one trying to resolve problems and looking for a solution. As a teacher leader, I mostly would want to accomplish the education of fellow teacher leaders on whatever topic I found to be my niche at any given point in my career. Many people do not have the time to look above the work that they have "in the trenches" and look for a way to make it even better. I would hope that I could be that person and that type of leader in my educational setting. (Angie, 2014)

My vision for myself regarding teacher leadership is to hopefully continue to lead within my classroom, at least for a few more years, while facilitating leadership opportunities for my fellow colleagues. . . . Sooner or later, I see myself leading in other capacities that aren't necessarily in the classroom but still affect students and learning. I really would like to accomplish leading teachers with best practices in hopes that we could work collaboratively for the sake of the students. I want others to describe me as a motivator and agent of change when it comes to being a teacher leader. I hope to be a catalyst for leading the right things within my school community. (Frankie, 2014).

WHAT ARE YOUR GOALS FOR TEACHER LEADERSHIP IN THE NEXT 1, 5, AND 10 YEARS?

Setting goals is related to developing a vision for oneself as a teacher leader. Because one's goals are typically included when completing a visioning activity, we think goal setting deserves more thought. We spend time on goal setting because we know it increases the ability of teachers to think metacognitively about teacher leadership, and we want teacher leaders to set both short-term and long-term goals that are concrete, realistic, and achievable. To keep goals true to life, we start by asking teacher leaders to create a timeline to show how they see their lives unfolding in the next 10 years. Because most teachers are female, we know that many of them have plans for their families as well as their careers. We also know from experience that once they see themselves as teacher leaders they often have new ideas about where they want to work or about getting more education. Figure 3.1 is an example of what a teacher leader's timeline might look like. Creating a timeline acknowledges teachers' real lives and ambitions and helps them be realistic about their goals, which Sheryl Nussbaum-Beach (2007) described so clearly in this blogpost:

> As teachers move through their careers they have different needs. How a teacher's personal life stage relates to their career stage has an influence on their willingness to serve as a teacher leader (Super et al., 1989). For example, very early in their careers teachers often do not have families and have the time to devote to cultivating leadership skills and serving in leadership roles within the school setting. A few years later, the onset of children might make staying for meetings and serving on committees difficult. Again, as teachers near retirement, caring for aging parents might interfere with taking on leadership roles. (n.p.)

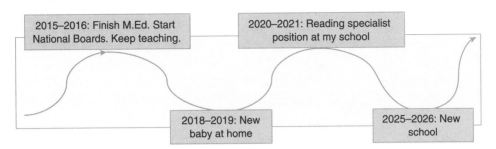

FIGURE 3.1   Sample Educator's Timeline: Level of Involvement in Teacher Leadership

2015–2016: Finish M.Ed. Start National Boards. Keep teaching.

2020–2021: Reading specialist position at my school

2018–2019: New baby at home

2025–2026: New school

When we ask teacher leaders to set explicit goals they want to accomplish in the next 1, 5, and 10 years, some goals have nothing to do with teacher leadership. We think this is okay because we want to acknowledge that everything teachers want to accomplish may not be related to school leadership. In fact, we encourage them to set both personal and professional goals. However, when they share their goals, we often find that we need to remind teachers that teacher leadership is not restricted to formal roles and responsibilities because often we see goals they don't recognize as leadership, but we do. Here are some examples of goals from teacher leaders we worked with recently:

A year from now, I see myself continuing to work closely with my grade level as grade-level chair and my content area. I see myself working with others to help the 8th grade and science department to run smoothly and reach goals. Five years from now, I see myself conducting professional development beyond the school in areas that I feel I may be an expert in. Ten years from now, I could see myself doing something more of a formal leadership role within the school or system whether it be teacher coach, curriculum coordinator, or the like. (Cory, 2014)

In one year, I will have become a mom (through adoption), so I will be taking some time off from teaching and teacher leadership. In five years, I see myself working in a teaching or administrative position (or a combination of both) that enables me to use my knowledge of effective reading instruction and my experience working with struggling adolescent readers. I would love to mentor teachers and provide professional development to help teachers increase reading achievement in their classrooms, particularly for their struggling readers. In ten years, I will be getting my PhD and doing research in the area of reading achievement and motivation for struggling adolescent readers. (Allison, 2014)

I do not plan on changing my role as a teacher leader in the next year. I enjoy my current role as a Service-Learning Teacher Leader, but I am not willing to take on additional roles without compensation. In five years, I think that

I will have taken on additional/different teacher leader roles. I am interested in honing my expertise as a writing teacher and working with other teachers in that capacity. I find that within my current department I am the most effective writing teacher because I spend the most time teaching writing. In ten years, I plan on moving on in my career and pursuing a PhD in Critical Disability Studies. I want to study the intersection of physical disability and education and become an advocate. Whether this advocacy comes through teaching or policy work or a combination I have not decided. (Katie, 2014)

It should be noted that Katie recently shortened her timeline and started her PhD program just 1 year after completing her teacher research and teacher leadership projects for her master's degree. Already a teacher leader, she will continue to demonstrate leadership in new areas.

WHAT IMAGE OR METAPHOR WOULD YOU CHOOSE FOR YOURSELF AS A TEACHER LEADER?

Dispositions are often revealed in the images and metaphors teacher leaders create for themselves. Pittman and O'Neill (2001) described the value of teachers evaluating their practice by creating metaphors, which we think applies equally to teacher leadership.

> Metaphors are powerful tools that teachers can use to examine their own beliefs about teaching and about themselves as teachers. When teachers choose metaphors to describe themselves, they attain deeper self-knowledge because those metaphors help express beliefs and understandings that are often tacit, implicit, and hidden from view. Only by openly expressing these beliefs and understandings can teachers begin to analyze them. (n.p.)

In addition, asking teachers to generate images and metaphors or similes that represent themselves as teacher leaders, or at least to reveal the current understanding of teacher leadership, requires them to use the right side of the brain (Sanders & Sanders, 1984). Clouse, Goodin, Aniello, McDowell, and McDowell (2013) stated, "Metaphor allows imagery (right brain) to be verbalized and creates imagery for specific facts (left brain)" (p. 83). We think this has value because almost all the other things we ask teacher leaders to do seem to privilege using the left-side of the brain. Therefore, we ask teacher leaders to choose a metaphor or simile for themselves as a teacher leader and to draw an image to accompany their metaphor. Sometimes we ask them to do one or the other, but not both; however, in all cases we ask for a written explanation of their metaphor or image. We often find that teacher leaders choose metaphors, or write similes, that describe how complex and challenging teacher leadership can be. For example, teacher leaders we know have described themselves as jugglers, orchestra conductors, circus ringmasters, and even as tightrope walkers and lion tamers. The circus theme is not always prevalent in every group we work with because other teacher leaders see themselves as gardeners or magicians who cultivate or conjure actions in others. We also get images like a spider web or a soaring eagle or the Energizer Bunny. Ironically, teacher-as-leader is a metaphor itself, as is teacher-as-researcher. The following is an example we provide them as a model for this task, which may account for all the circus metaphors we received recently.

> As a teacher leader I am a juggler who is always juggling multiple hats while keeping multiple balls in the air. I am perpetually in motion and try to balance many things at the same time. I chose a juggler as my metaphor for teacher leadership because I feel teacher leaders take on many roles both inside and outside their classroom and have to be and do many things and move constantly to accomplish everything they want to see happen.

WHAT OBSTACLES DO YOU NEED TO OVERCOME TO BECOME A STRONG TEACHER LEADER?

Often the discussions we have about their metaphors or images as teacher leaders lead into discussions about the complex nature and the challenges of teacher leadership. When asked about obstacles to teacher leadership, Cameron's response captures several obstacles that concern most teachers.

> *There are a few pitfalls that come to mind with teacher leaders. (1) Balancing teacher leadership roles with your personal life can be extremely difficult. Individuals have to be prepared to balance each so that the stress does not affect their lives. (2) Another situation is when teacher leaders are not supported by administrators. Without this support, it can be near impossible to accomplish things for your department and/or teachers. (3) Another pitfall is when someone views the position as a type of personal gain. Viewing teacher leadership positions as a personal gain changes your vision while you are in the position. Your sights are moved from where they should be: student success, teacher success, and school success. (4) Finally, working with peers while in a leadership role can create tensions that were not there before. Individuals may treat you differently, possibly resent you, for your new position of power. If peers do not support you, they may not be supportive in your move to change.*

This kind of reflection leads to further discussion and an activity we use to help teachers think about how they can overcome some of the challenges they might face. However, many of the solutions to the challenges teachers face, with the exception of the ubiquitous lack of time, often have to do with their disposition about adversity. An activity we use engages teachers in small groups to list challenges to teacher leadership and then to brainstorm possible ways to overcome each obstacle or challenge on their list. Usually someone in the group can think of possible ways to overcome a challenge they or others face, which is why we always do this as a group activity. Nevertheless, first we ask teachers to list challenges and possible ways to overcome them, and then we ask them to share with others so we can create a composite T-chart that often looks like Table 3.3.

TABLE 3.3 Ways to Overcome Obstacles to Teacher Leadership

OBSTACLES TO TEACHER LEADERSHIP	POSSIBLE WAYS TO OVERCOME THESE OBSTACLES
• Lack of support from my principal	• Request a face-to-face meeting • Have an agenda and/or questions prepared ahead of any meeting • Initiate specific discussions about roles, needs, outcomes, plans, and resources • Be sure you and the administrator are on the same page • Take a willing partner with you—for support and as another voice • Remain professional—do not gossip or complain • Respect and understand your principal's constraints and responsibilities—try to see the big picture • Develop your own support network • Join a professional teacher organization/union just in case there is a grievance
• Lack of support from other teachers	• Seek feedback and take suggestions from other teachers openly and willingly • Ask teachers what they need or want to happen • Find willing partners—never try to go it alone • Make sure all communications are clear and not just one-way • Be sure to build and maintain trusting relationships • Exercise democratic values when presenting any project to peers • Talk to teacher(s) directly about whatever the concern is • Provide materials that will be helpful • Offer to cover or trade duties when other teachers are helping out • Remain positive and professional • Seek support from administrators • Ask someone to mediate
• Don't know what to do—have no/little related professional development or experience	• Ask someone for information and/or assistance • Read online • Find a collaborator who does know what to do • Just try your best, but be realistic • Know your strengths and use them to help yourself • Choose a leadership role that will not seem like work • Ask to be a coleader or cochair for a year

EVERY TEACHER A LEADER   https://resources.corwin.com/everyteacheraleader

OBSTACLES TO TEACHER LEADERSHIP	POSSIBLE WAYS TO OVERCOME THESE OBSTACLES
	• Ask to attend a workshop or conference
	• Subscribe to and read a professional journal
	• Consider doing a teacher action research project to learn
• Resistance from others about learning/doing new things	• Listen carefully to everyone's concerns
	• Include others in the planning process
	• Assess the school culture
	• Make decisions based on the best ways to maintain a healthy working environment
	• Be patient
	• Don't ask for too much at any one time
	• Find or develop allies
	• Make the change or new program a pilot—like a trial run that can be re-evaluated
	• Understand how people react to change and meet them where they are
	• Give choices whenever and wherever possible

HOW CAN YOU OVERCOME OBSTACLES TO TEACHER LEADERSHIP?

Any discussion of obstacles to teacher leadership, and ways to overcome them, comes back to dispositions as well as knowledge and skills, as can be seen in Table 3.3. This leads us to further discussion or review of possible goals for overcoming perceived or real obstacles to becoming a strong teacher leader. When asked to write about overcoming obstacles to teacher leadership, two recent teacher leaders we worked with summarized their thinking in ways we think offer wise advice to other teacher leaders.

> *Common obstacles and pitfalls, such as choosing/accepting a leadership role, relationships, working with colleagues, and facilitating learning, can be overcome in a variety of ways. The first is to choose a leadership role that will not seem like work—this will decrease the potential of burnout, a common TL pitfall. Along the same line in choosing a leadership role, maintaining a balance between personal and professional life will keep burnout at bay. A second obstacle to teacher leadership is relationships with colleagues. Resentment of success and conformity to the flat structure of teaching can keep peers resistant to working with teacher leaders. Teacher leaders can overcome this resentment by providing resources, finding common ground, reminding teachers they are just facilitating as equals—and keeping any feedback positive. A final obstacle, and one that I connect most with, is the need for quality professional development. Often the school-based PD does not reflect the concerns of the teachers, so*

one way to overcome this is to seek out your own PD. I have done this by attending national and state conferences, maintaining a subscription to the English Journal, *and aligning my Professional Development Plan with my own interests as they connect to the School Improvement Plan.* (Katie, 2014)

I can imagine that teacher leaders will encounter many challenges. I feel that one of the best ways to overcome these is by having a support group or core group of people in the school who are also teacher leaders. This is the best way to release frustrations, to discuss strategies, and to also form unity among the teacher leaders. This may help in creating "buy-in" when teacher leaders are in need of support. Another way to overcome obstacles is to have support from administrators, whether it be financially, administratively, or even just for moral support. If teacher leaders do not have administrator support, they will find it difficult to overcome challenges. Another important way to overcome challenges and pitfalls would be refreshing and energizing teacher leaders. It is important to allow teacher leaders to attend conferences, seminars, or even meetings with other teacher leaders such as the Triad Teacher Researcher event. This can be a great way to get new ideas, to energize them, and refresh their efforts. Administrators need to keep this in mind and perhaps even allow for extra days off work for these events. I think these three items can really help teacher leaders overcome challenges or pitfalls they are experiencing. (Angie, 2014)

SUMMARY

In this chapter, we discussed dispositions needed by teacher leaders, how to establish a vision and set goals for teacher leadership, and ways to build self-efficacy for teacher leadership. We also addressed obstacles to successful teacher leadership and ways to ameliorate these obstacles. The voices of teacher leaders included in this chapter offer authentic reactions to how they understand and address obstacles to teacher leadership and how they see their visions and goals as teacher leaders. Several opportunities for personal assessment and self-analysis are included in this chapter, as well as activities to encourage teacher leaders to recognize all the ways they lead both formally and informally inside and outside their classrooms and schools. Additional activities, readings, and scenarios, and questions for reflection and discussion are available in the companion website for this book.

CHAPTER 4

What Teacher Leaders Need to Know

Leadership does not mean that we become a different person; rather we become more of the person we could become. This allows us to do and change many things.

(Martin Woolnough, www.guide-to-managing-change.com)

VIEW FROM A SCHOOL LEADER	VIEW FROM A TEACHER LEADER
Mrs. Brown, I think you are ready to be a leader now. I see that you have very good communication skills, are organized, and seem well able to set and adjust your goals as needed. You also seem to be able to think metacognitively about your teaching when I talk with you after an observation. I think you work equally well with students and adults, which is important for a teacher leader to be able to do.	*Thanks for your encouragement, Mr. Peterson, but I don't exactly know what you mean when you say I seem to think metacognitively about my teaching. What does that mean? And what does that have to do with being a mentor and serving on the school improvement team? Of course, I love working with students, but I don't have as much knowledge about how to work with adults as I do with our students.*

This chapter focuses on important knowledge needed for teacher leadership. The first thing teacher leaders need to know is about themselves as learners and leaders, so this is where we begin. We start with self-knowledge because we believe meta-cognition is important for teacher leaders to develop. Other knowledge in this chapter includes understanding adult learners and their needs and knowing how teachers develop throughout their careers. Armed with such information, teacher leaders will be more knowledgeable about themselves and others; hence they will be better able to lead. We address additional knowledge teacher leaders need in Chapter 5, but the questions answered in this chapter include:

1. What do teacher leaders need to know about themselves?

2. What supports metacognitive thinking as a teacher leader?

3. How can understanding the needs of adults help teacher leaders?

4. How can teacher leaders work best with different generations?

5. Why is understanding teacher development important to our efforts as teacher leaders?

WHAT DO TEACHER LEADERS NEED TO KNOW ABOUT THEMSELVES?

We, and others (e.g., Katzenmeyer & Moller, 2009), think that teacher leaders must be knowledgeable about who they are and who they want to become. Teacher leaders we have worked with concur that self-knowledge is important, and understand that without self-knowledge they may not be attuned to the diversity of their colleagues, or respect how others approach learning new things or think about teacher leadership. It is important, as Lindsay (2013), one of the teacher leaders we worked with, recently wrote:

> For teacher leaders to not only understand themselves but also be understanding of the views and beliefs of others. Teachers must first be self-aware of who they are as educators before they can gain the support of others. Self-awareness as a teacher involves knowing how one's previous experiences, personal life, and teaching experiences have shaped who they are as teachers. Recognition of this sense of self will then allow teachers to obtain a deeper understanding of the school environment in which they work and access to others' ideals and beliefs. Teacher leaders must reflect on these ideas and be willing to understand that others may not always share these same ideas. . . . It is important for teacher leaders to be conscious of their surroundings and not only understand but also celebrate the differences that exist among teachers. Recognizing all of these factors will help influence school change on a broader scale and increase students' successes.

Few would argue that the beliefs teachers hold influence their perceptions, judgments, and dispositions. Teachers' beliefs also influence their behaviors, decisions, and actions (Levin, 2014). Understanding one's beliefs related to teaching and teacher leadership is an important step in developing as a teacher leader. Furthermore, making one's beliefs explicit allows them to be open and available for conscious examination and action. Conversely, when beliefs remain implicit and unexamined, they may yield unintended or undesired actions or reactions. Further, we would argue that knowing what their teachers believe will allow school leaders, professional development (PD) leaders, and other mentors to help potential teacher leaders develop the dispositions, knowledge, and skills they need to be successful teacher leaders.

While beliefs are different than knowledge, and this chapter is about knowledge needed by teacher leaders, we think it is important to address teachers' beliefs because they are part of knowing oneself and because beliefs guide teachers' practical knowledge and their behaviors (Levin, 2014; Verloop, Van Driel, & Meijer, 2001). Beliefs also serve as a filter through which teachers view knowledge (Fives & Buehl, 2012; Levin, 2014; Richardson, 2003), which includes knowledge they need to be teacher leaders. Pajares (1992) suggested that although teachers may conflate knowledge and beliefs, the distinction is that beliefs are more personal, whereas knowledge is based on objective facts agreed upon by particular communities (Richardson, 1996, 2003). Also, much of what is considered professional knowledge has been categorized as beliefs (Kagan, 1992).

In our practice, one way we help teacher leaders begin to develop self-knowledge is by asking them to make their strongly held beliefs explicit—thus available for examination by themselves and others. We do this by engaging teachers in a personal theorizing process to elicit their beliefs by generating what we, and others, have called personal practical theories, or PPTs (Levin, 2014; Lundeberg & Levin, 2003). Based on Cornett's (1990) early work on teacher beliefs, we define PPTs as *teachers' beliefs that guide their classroom practices (theories) based on prior life experiences, including nonteaching activities (personal), and experiences that occur as a result of designing and teaching the curriculum (practical).* Helping teachers uncover, explicitly state, and then study the ways they enact their beliefs increases their self-knowledge, can help them develop metacognitive thinking about teacher leadership, and supports their developing sense of agency as teacher leaders. We describe a process for increasing teachers' self-knowledge by eliciting their beliefs in the following activity.

> *Personal practical theories are teachers' beliefs that guide their classroom practices (theories) based on prior life experiences, including nonteaching activities (personal), and experiences that occur as a result of designing and teaching the curriculum (practical).*

ACTIVITY: Engaging in the personal theorizing process will help you think about and articulate your tacit beliefs and make them explicit, either orally or in writing. In the context of supporting your development as a teacher leader, the personal theorizing process can be accomplished in three steps:

1. First, one's personal practical theories (PPTs) are a manifestation of one's strongly held beliefs about teachers, teaching, students, learning, school, curriculum, and both school and teacher leadership, for example. Some examples

(Continued)

(Continued)

of PPTs are provided at the end of this activity, but first complete the following sentences to jumpstart your thinking about your beliefs related to teacher leadership:

- I am at my best when . . .
- Students say they like me when . . .
- Friends/family say I am . . .
- Supervisors think that I . . .
- I love leading when . . .
- The things on which I agree with my colleagues are . . .

2. Second, reflect on and write down what you personally believe is important to you about teaching and leadership. Think about what leadership is, what teacher leadership means to you, what you think leading would look like in action, and the connections you see between teaching and leadership and between teachers and leaders. Also reflect on and write down what leadership is not, ways you see yourself acting or doing things as a teacher leader, and what knowledge and skills you think you need to be an effective teacher and teacher leader.

3. Third, develop 5 to 8 statements that express what you believe about teaching and teacher leadership. Use only I-statements (e.g., I believe that as a teacher leader I can only be successful by collaborating with others) rather than statements about what others might say about teacher leadership or what teacher leaders should do (e.g., Teacher leaders should collaborate with others, or Teacher leadership is about collaboration). This is important because everyone's PPTs are uniquely personal. However, be prepared to share your PPTs with others in small or large groups, and listen to see if there are any shared beliefs in the group.

Some examples of PPTs, or beliefs, about teacher leadership include the following:

- I have high expectations for my students and myself as a leader.
- I believe that all students can learn and it is my responsibility to ensure this happens. I think this is my primary responsibility as a teacher leader.
- I believe that students need to know how what they are learning applies to their lives. Therefore, I believe in making real-world connections in my teaching.
- I think that communicating effectively with students, parents, and colleagues is key to everything I want to accomplish as a teacher leader.
- I always try to empathize with both my students and colleagues and develop genuine relationships. I believe that relationships are key to teacher leadership.
- I believe that collaboration is a very important key to my success as a teacher and a teacher leader.

We also ask the teacher leaders we work with to use their beliefs statements, or PPTs, about teacher leadership as a foundation for teacher research, which we address in Chapter 5, or any teacher leadership projects they might want to undertake. We do this so they have grounded, purposeful reasons for choosing particular teacher research or leadership projects based on their beliefs versus what others might suggest to them.

There are many other ways to elicit teacher beliefs, including writing narratives, autobiographies, life histories, and metaphors. Explicating one's teaching philosophy, or more specifically writing about one's philosophy of leadership is also a good way to surface beliefs. This and other reflective activities to reveal teachers' beliefs about leadership are described in the online guide that accompanies this book.

WHAT SUPPORTS METACOGNITIVE THINKING AS A TEACHER LEADER?

Aside from articulating your beliefs as a teacher, and especially your beliefs about teacher leadership, exercising other ways to increase self-knowledge will also increase your ability to think metacognitively about teacher leadership. We want teacher leaders to be purposeful about their leadership, to have self-knowledge about the strengths and skills they possess, and to understand what they still need to learn to be successful leaders.

Metacognition is about awareness and understanding of one's own thought processes. Metacognition is a type of higher-order thinking that enables awareness, analysis, and command of your cognitive thought processes, especially when you are engaged in learning. In sum, being able to think metacognitively means that you are aware of what you know and what you don't know, you also understand what you might need to know or learn to accomplish a particular task, and you are able to use what you already know to accomplish a task.

Teachers who lead have a lot of demands placed on their time, so they must think and act smartly. Therefore, they need to think metacognitively and help other teachers use metacognition purposefully. In other words, teacher leaders must have self-knowledge about what they and others have learned, and understand how they learned to direct their own learning and that of others.

Actually, even first-year teachers engage in high levels of metacognitive thinking virtually all the time because everything is new (Duffy, Miller, Parsons, & Meloth, 2007); the same thing happens to all teachers when the curriculum changes, or when new concepts or a new program is introduced. However, teacher leaders need to be aware of their own preferred ways of teaching and learning so that they don't fall into the trap of limiting the ways they work with other teachers based on their own preferences. For example, if I know that I learn best by reading and taking notes, I also need to know that others may learn by seeing examples in action on a video, or by observing in real time. Others may need to actually try out a new idea before they really understand it, so I cannot limit my efforts as a teacher leader to just offering readings or expecting people to take notes.

Reflection and self-regulation are two key aspects of metacognition. Reflection is the act of thinking about what we think we know, while self-regulation has to do with being able to organize and manage how we will continue to learn. Developing metacognition is not just about becoming a reflective practitioner; it is also about developing specific strategies that are useful knowledge for teacher leaders to have. Metacognition includes planning and organizing activities, setting goals, being aware of one's performance throughout a task, self-monitoring, and directing processes and strategies that are needed to make progress toward achieving one's goals. Metacognition requires self-assessment and critical self-reflection.

Metacognition is a close cousin to critical thinking and problem solving, and understanding why and when to use a particular strategy. Fortunately, specific steps to develop metacognitive thinking can be taken by teacher leaders. These include setting goals or targets, dividing big tasks into smaller tasks, creating timelines, checking one's progress on the timeline, and troubleshooting when problems or roadblocks arise. Troubleshooting can include checking progress toward one's goals, focusing and paying attention to the task at hand, asking others for help when needed, and advocating for oneself when necessary. Being willing to adjust and actually make any needed adjustments or modification is also a hallmark of metacognitive thinking. Reflection can and should include consciously and critically assessing both successful and unsuccessful strategies and thinking ahead about how to adjust both time and strategies needed for future goals.

Some concrete ways teacher leaders can develop their own metacognitive thinking include establishing a vision for themselves as teacher leaders, setting goals, and developing timelines, as discussed in Chapter 3. Self-questioning, reflective journal writing, and discussing your thought processes with other teacher leaders are additional ways teacher leaders can exercise their metacognitive processes. In the ideal situation, a teacher leader can partner regularly with another educator to have this type of dialogue and support. However, we consciously teach and talk explicitly about what metacognition is, how and why teacher leaders should work to develop this kind of self-knowledge, and how they can use metacognitive strategies to help students they teach as well other teachers they work with in a leadership capacity. Further, we hope school leaders will create opportunities for teachers and teacher leaders to engage in this type of behavior by adjusting how time is used in meetings and throughout the school day or week.

ACTIVITY: To evaluate your growing understanding of metacognition, think about and then write or discuss your responses to these questions: What do you now understand

---

about metacognition? What do you not understand? What else would you like to know about metacognition? How might you go about learning more about metacognition? Why do you think metacognition is important for teacher leaders to develop? How can you use what you know about metacognition to develop as a teacher leader? What metacognitive strategies could you use when problems or dilemmas arise in your classroom or school? How will you know if these strategies worked? Alternatively, write at least five (5) things you learned about metacognition, at least three metacognitive strategies you plan to add to your repertoire, and at least one question you still have about metacognition.

In addition to using the information and strategies described above to help teacher leaders develop their metacognitive abilities, the questions asked in Table 4.1 are another way for you to assess and evaluate the strength of your understanding and use of metacognition. Using a scale of 1 (low or rarely) to 4 (high or often), you should rate yourself on each of these questions related to metacognition and your disposition toward this kind of thinking. Total scores of 80–100 are an indication of strong understanding and use of metacognitive thinking, while scores of 60–79 are average, and scores of 40–59 are lower than average, which indicates a need for targeted efforts. When low scores are encountered, you should set goals to increase your metacognitive thinking by choosing some of the strategies described above.

TABLE 4.1   Assessing Your Understanding and Use of Metacognitive Thinking

QUESTIONS	1	2	3	4
1. What is your level of knowledge about how human beings learn?	1	2	3	4
2. How well do you understand your own learning processes?	1	2	3	4
3. How self-efficacious do you feel?	1	2	3	4
4. How self-confident are you?	1	2	3	4
5. What is your sense of agency?	1	2	3	4
6. How flexible or adaptable are you?	1	2	3	4
7. How often do you think strategically?	1	2	3	4
8. How often do you seek out partners or allies?	1	2	3	4
9. Are you a decision maker?	1	2	3	4
10. Are you a consensus builder?	1	2	3	4
11. Is reflection a habit for you?	1	2	3	4

(Continued)

TABLE 4.1   (Continued)

QUESTIONS	1	2	3	4
12. Do you have a vision for how the tasks you set will work?	1	2	3	4
13. How skilled are you about defining tasks to be completed?	1	2	3	4
14. Can you figure out steps for completing tasks that need to be accomplished?	1	2	3	4
15. How well do you typically execute plans to complete tasks?	1	2	3	4
16. How good are you at self-monitoring to complete tasks?	1	2	3	4
17. Do you see problems as opportunities?	1	2	3	4
18. How often do you seek assistance?	1	2	3	4
19. Are you a do-it-myself person?	1	2	3	4
20. Are you aware of both what you know and do not know?	1	2	3	4
21. How consistent are you with making plans?	1	2	3	4
22. How strategic are you when making decisions?	1	2	3	4
23. How often do you evaluate your plans (before, during, after)?	1	2	3	4
24. How well can you detect errors and correct them?	1	2	3	4
25. Are you willing to shift and change/revise strategies?	1	2	3	4
Sum the number of checks in each column, and multiple by column number (1–4). Add all column totals to get a final score.	1	2	3	4

HOW CAN UNDERSTANDING THE NEEDS OF ADULTS HELP TEACHER LEADERS?

In addition to teacher leaders increasing their self-knowledge by learning about metacognition and using metacognitive strategies, understanding how adults learn is important knowledge for teacher leaders. Such knowledge helps teacher leaders better understand themselves and their colleagues. It is practical knowledge they can apply when working with other adults. Furthermore, because teacher leaders will likely work with adults who are either older or younger than themselves, we think knowledge about the characteristics and preferences of different generations is important knowledge for teacher leaders. Given that during their teacher preparation program most teachers only learned about child and adolescent development, teachers we work with are very interested in learning more about working effectively with adults. However, we also find that they already know a lot about themselves as adult learners, so we always ask them to brainstorm and share what their best professional learning opportunities have been. We ask them to think about what they like and do not like when they attend a workshop, a conference presentation, a class, or any other PD opportunity they have experienced. As it turns out, articulating what they prefer as adult learners almost always mirrors what the literature says about adults.

There is a whole field of study about adult learners called *andragogy* (e.g., Knowles, 1980; Merriam, Caffarella, & Baumgartner, 2007). Basic assumptions in the literature about adult learners include these characteristics: They are typically more self-directed in their learning; their past experiences serve as a resource to support their learning; their motivation to learn is usually intrinsic; they are focused on solving problems; and they appreciate learning things that are relevant and have practical application to their real life. Because the basic tenets of andragogy relate to meeting the needs of adult learners, we think teacher leaders should not only be knowledgeable about them but also cater to them in their work as a teacher leader. In Table 4.2, we summarize some ways to use what we know about the needs of adult learners.

TABLE 4.2   Ways to Meet the Needs of Adult Learners

- Acknowledge and make use of their prior knowledge and experiences:
  - Ask what they already know
  - Provide time to share examples and experiences
  - Explicitly acknowledge their expertise

- Recognize the need for affiliation and connection:
  - Put them into groups
  - Do warm-up activities and ask for personal introductions
  - Help them make personal connections
  - Highlight things they might relate to personally

- Make learning active and interactive:
  - Make them do the thinking and the work
  - Have them talk to each other regularly
  - Engage them in finding, discussing, and solving problems
  - Allow them to debate, reflect, write, discuss scenarios, and so on

- Recognize that everyone has different learning styles:
  - Provide learning opportunities that will appeal to visual learners, auditory learners, kinesthetic learners
  - Consider having them take a learning style inventory
  - Make use of other self-assessments

As mentioned above, we encourage teacher leaders to cater to the needs of adult learners. That is, teacher leaders would be wise to first reflect on what they, as adults, find most useful to their own learning, and then use what they already know about themselves as adult learners when working with other adults. This includes rethinking how they might teach adults in comparison to how they teach children. Teacher leaders should consciously and purposefully consider both the roles they will take on when working with other adults (see Table 4.3 for examples) and how they might plan for adult learning when leading professional learning opportunities, for example, which we describe in Table 4.4.

TABLE 4.3   Roles for Teacher Leaders When Leading Adults

- **Learning Facilitator . . .**
  - Help adult learners develop their own learning objectives
  - Choose appropriate strategies for learning
  - Provide appropriate content and new information
- **Resource Advisor . . .**
  - Share materials
  - Offer personal examples
  - Provide new or additional resources
- **Teacher . . .**
  - Acknowledge complexity and ambiguity
  - Discuss the complexities and nuances of your topic
  - Do not oversimplify things
  - Assess what participants are learning
- **Teacher Leader . . .**
  - Share power and authority for making decisions whenever possible
  - Offer choices
  - Share the stage
  - Have others present with you

TABLE 4.4   Practical Tips for Teacher Leaders Leading Adult Learners

- Do a needs assessment (see Chapter 7 for detailed information)
  - Adjust your plans based on the results
- Select manageable aspects to focus on given the amount of time available
  - Be flexible and adapt your plans as needed
- Make goals and objectives explicit
- Share plans for session/workshop
  - Ask for other items to add to the agenda
- Provide handouts—and food!
- Invite questions
  - Be gracious with contrasting viewpoints
- Be sure your questions include HOTS (higher-order thinking skills)
- Use "inter-activities" that are authentic and relevant
- Provide video examples whenever possible
- Include time for processing
  - Small- and large-group discussion times
  - Written reflection
  - Formative assessment
- Ask everyone to commit to trying something—to taking action
- Give breaks

Knowing that the needs of adult learners may be different than what teachers already know about children's learning needs, we think a crucial ingredient in teaching adults effectively is attention to planning. This includes identifying the needs of the group, carefully considering the appropriate time and setting for learning together, setting clear goals and objectives (and sharing these publicly), planning "inter-active" activities, and being sure to assess what is learned during each professional learning opportunity. In addition, it is important for a teacher leader to be willing to modify plans based on the needs and interests of the adults you work with. Inflexible plans can become an impediment to progress. So being flexible is key when working with adults!

HOW CAN TEACHER LEADERS WORK BEST WITH DIFFERENT GENERATIONS?

Today's schools include faculty and staff covering four generations. Teacher leaders may come from any one of these generations, and you will likely work with teachers from many different generations at the same time. These generations include the Baby Boomers who are our veteran teachers and school leaders born between mid-1940s and mid-1960s, and Gen Xers born between the mid-1960s and the mid-1980s. These two generations may already be serving as school and teacher leaders. However, Baby Boomers only account for about 12% of today's workforce, while Gen Xers account for 43% of the workforce. We also have Gen Y, more popularly called the Millennials, born between the mid-1980s and early 2000s. They account for 44% of today's workforce, the largest pool of current and future teacher leaders. And then there are the Gen Zers, born between 2000 and 2020 who will soon be our newest teachers and leaders. Each of these generations, as a group, had different experiences and expectations growing up, which affects their view of the world (Zemke, Raines, & Filipczak, 2013), although generational views may overlap—especially for people born within 7 or 8 years at either end of a generation.

> Regardless of who we are and where we grew up, the common features within generations cut across racial, ethnic, cultural and economic differences. As unique as people's individual experiences may be, they share a place in history with all members of their generation. All members of a generation have been influenced by the world events, music, technology, heroes and catastrophes that occurred during their most formative years. (Arnsparger, 2008, n.p.)

Differences in generational groups, though perhaps not for every individual in a generational group, means it is important to know how to lead them in different ways. For example, many Baby Boomers and Gen Xers are not as tech savvy as either Millennials or Gen Zers, so they may not be excited about using technology to work on leadership issues or as a teaching and learning tool. Many Baby Boomers are used to top-down management, are very work-oriented, and many have willingly sacrificed some of their personal time for their job. However, most

Millennials, now the largest generation in today's workforce, are serious about finding a better work-life balance than their parents (Zemke et al., 2013). Millennials as a group are looking for leaders who are honest and have integrity, and they want challenges, opportunities for growth, and a career path that might include teacher leadership (Schrum & Levin, 2009, 2015). They also like to work cooperatively and have fun along the way (Zemke et al., 2013). In fact, we believe that members of all generations may want these same things and also want to be treated respectfully, have their ideas considered thoughtfully, and receive feedback and recognition. However, each generation may desire to be recognized differently. For example, "Generation Y is less likely to respond well to traditional recognition such as a certificate or plaque for their office wall.... If you want to recognise the new generation give them a half-day off or provide a free car wash coupon" (Hughes & Fiehl, 2013, p. 46).

> All generations may want these same things and also want to be treated respectfully, have their ideas considered thoughtfully, and receive feedback and recognition.

As a way to summarize some key knowledge that teacher leaders need to have about different generations, Table 4.5 provides information about the strengths of three generations (Boomers, Gen Xer, and Millennials), as well as what motivates them. We offer this information to further develop your knowledge base for teacher leadership. However, it is also important for teacher leaders to recognize what all generations have in common:

- Work is a vehicle for personal fulfillment and satisfaction, not just for a paycheck.
- Workplace culture is important.
- Being trusted to get the job done is the number one factor that defines job satisfaction.
- They need to feel valued by their employer to be happy in the job.
- They want flexibility in the workplace.
- Success is finding a company they can stay with for a long time.
- Career development is the most valued form of recognition, even more so than pay raises and enhanced titles. (Arnsparger, 2008, n.p.)

In sum, knowledge of the similarities and differences among generations is important to successful leadership. Not only does this knowledge help teacher leaders understand others, but it also helps them better understand themselves and their peers. As we have focused on self-knowledge in this chapter, we think it would be valuable for teacher leaders to explicitly acknowledge and then leverage generational differences, especially capitalizing on generational strengths, as long as they are careful not to stereotype others.

TABLE 4.5   Strengths and Motivations of Boomers, Gen Xers, and Millennials

	BABY BOOMERS	GEN XERS	MILLENNIALS
Strengths	• Committed to customer service • Dedicated • Good team members • Optimistic • Future-oriented • A wealth of experience and knowledge	• Adaptable • Technologically literate • Independent • Creative • Expect to contribute • Willing to buck the system	• Optimistic • Able to multi-task • Technologically savvy • A global worldview • Goal and achievement-oriented • Believe in volunteerism and serving their communities
What Motivates Them	• Leaders who get them involved and show them how they can make a difference • Managers who value their opinion and recognize their contributions	• Giving them the freedom to get the job done on their own schedule • Allowing them to do it their way • Having very few rules • Being more informal than "corporate"	• Managers who connect their actions to their personal and career goals • The promise of working with other bright, creative people • Having adequate time and flexibility to live the life they want

SOURCE: Arnsparger, 2008, n.p.

ACTIVITY: Read some online articles about generational differences (www.genera tionsatwork.com), or review the information above about the characteristics of different generations and how to work with them. Self-identify what generation you most associate with. Make a Venn diagram or list points of similarity and points of difference across generational groups to make their characteristics explicit and open to further examination. Now think about a recent PD experience and respond to these questions:

- Do you think the presenters were able to meet the needs of the adult learners from different generations?

- Did they focus more on the learning needs of one generation? Was it your generation?

- In retrospect, what could you do that would better meet intergenerational educators' needs when you next work with other adults?

Discuss these questions with peers, if possible. Finally, review the list of genera-tional strengths and motivations in Table 4.5 and make a commitment to consider this new knowledge when forming teams, working in groups, giving feedback and rewards, planning for PD, and solving conflicts.

WHY IS UNDERSTANDING TEACHER DEVELOPMENT IMPORTANT TO OUR EFFORTS AS TEACHER LEADERS?

In addition to knowledge about the needs of adult learners and understanding generational differences, we have found that teacher leaders benefit from research-based knowledge about how teachers develop throughout their careers. Knowledge about how teachers develop is rarely shared during teacher preparation, but we find the teacher leaders are very interested in their own development as a teacher and how researchers describe teacher development. Fortunately, or unfortunately, there are several cognitive theories of teacher development, but there is no single theory with which everyone agrees. There are several models of how teachers begin to develop (Kagan, 1992) and what their concerns are early in their careers (e.g., Fuller, 1969; Fuller & Brown, 1975). These early concerns, typically felt before and during the early months of their first teaching job, are about themselves, how others will view them, and whether they will be accepted. This is followed by concerns about teaching the curriculum well. Finally, teachers' concerns shift to focus on their students and concerns about meeting their students' needs and teaching them well. Typically, concerns about students are the focus of beginning teachers by the end of their first year, and continue to be the focus for most teachers, or they drop out.

Next, we share two models of teacher development that cover the life span of teachers' careers (see Levin, 2003, for summaries of additional models of teacher development). These models describe how teachers' pedagogical knowledge develops over time. One model describes how teachers' thinking and their focus shift in the classroom as they develop from novices into experts (Berliner, 1986, 1988) based on information processing theory. The other model describes the development of teachers' pedagogical thinking across the career span (Levin, 2003) based on developmental stage theory. Unfortunately, there is no theory or model that captures the complexity of teachers' thinking or that addresses all the domains of what teachers have to learn and teach, including how they might become teacher leaders. However, these models were based on extensive observations and interviews of teachers across the career span; that is, they are empirically based and not just theoretical.

The information we share here is offered to help teachers become more knowledgeable about themselves. In other words, these models have heuristic value because they help teachers think about and self-assess where they are developmentally so that they might think about how they may continue to develop. These models of teacher development also provide information that teacher leaders need to know about the developmental needs of other teachers they work with in a leadership capacity. This knowledge may be especially useful for those engaged in mentoring new teachers.

Berliner and his colleagues (1986, 1988) used schema theory and posited five stages of novice to expert teacher cognition about classroom practices to offer a model of how pedagogical expertise develops in the classroom. This model of teacher development emphasizes the role of experience in understanding different views of pedagogy held by teachers in novice thru expert stages. It also indicates that teachers may begin to think metacognitively about their classroom practices as early as their third or fourth year in the classroom.

1. Novice—Preservice and first-year teachers learn to do commonplace teaching tasks through real-world experience, and make context-free rules ("Don't smile until Christmas") and decisions; minimal skill is displayed.

2. Advanced beginner—Second- and third-year teachers begin developing episodic and strategic knowledge, but context now comes into play when making decisions. Advanced beginners may not know when to break or to follow rules and procedures, and may not have a sense of what is important.

3. Competent—As early as their third or fourth year, teachers begin to make conscious decisions, are able to prioritize and set goals, and display control of the classroom and the curriculum. Competent teachers are able to distinguish between what is and is not important and do not usually make timing or targeting errors. They also feel more personally in control of the classroom events and their curriculum.

4. Proficient—Proficiency emerges in the fifth year for a modest number of teachers who are able to strategically analyze and make conscious decisions (i.e., think metacognitively). Their intuition and know-how are more developed and can be more easily applied. Proficient teachers recognize similarities in situations they have used before and can predict events. They are analytical and deliberate in their decision making.

5. Expert—Expert teachers are characterized by thoughts and actions that are fluid, flexible, and flowing. Unless a problem develops, they do not have to be consciously analytic or think deliberately about their pedagogical decisions because many practices have become automatized. They are quick to recognize a problem and deliberately analyze it.

The second model, the Ammon and Hutcheson Model of Pedagogical Development (see Levin, 2003), is a developmental, stage model that addresses four aspects of pedagogy—teachers' thinking about teaching, learning, behavior, and children's development. In its simplest form it focuses on how teachers develop their thinking and what they understand about teaching and learning over time. This model includes six developmental markers of pedagogical practice that are cumulative and inclusive of previous ways of thinking, but also successively more sophisticated at each level. Therefore, it is important to reiterate that developing a more sophisticated view of teaching and learning does not mean abandoning previous practices; they are included, but the higher level of thinking becomes the newer and now fundamental way of understanding teaching and learning.

1. Naïve Empiricism—Teaching is essentially showing and telling students what they need to know in ways that are appealing. Learning comes from experiencing.

2. Everyday Behaviorism—Teaching is essentially modeling and reinforcing. Learning comes from students doing, practicing, and drilling.

3. Global Constructivism—Teaching is essentially providing hands-on experiences. Learning comes from students having many opportunities to explore.

4. Differentiated Constructivism—Teaching is essentially guiding students' thinking within domains. Learning comes from students engaging in sense making.

5. Integrated Constructivism—Teaching is engaging students in challenging activities and guiding their understanding across several domains. Learning comes from students engaging in problem solving.

6. Connected Constructivism—Teaching is engaging students in challenging activities and encouraging their metacognitive awareness and understanding of academic, social, and ethical issues and concepts inherent in every domain. Learning comes from students' self-awareness and taking responsibility for their own thinking and learning.

As mentioned above, both these models were developed based on interviewing and observing teachers in action in their classrooms, but longitudinal research (Levin, 2003) found that three important factors influence teacher development: (1) opportunities for ongoing, high-quality PD; (2) provision made for personal and professional support; and (3) the ability to be reflective and think metacognitively. Based on these findings, it seems logical that teacher leaders also need ongoing, high-quality professional learning opportunities, personal and professional support, and to think reflectively and to develop the ability to think metacognitively if they are going to develop throughout their careers as teacher leaders.

SUMMARY

In this chapter we focused on self-knowledge needed by current and future teacher leaders, as well as by school leaders encouraging teacher leaders. To increase teacher leaders' self-knowledge, we discussed the importance of identifying one's beliefs through a personal theorizing process, and the importance of learning how to think metacognitively as a teacher leader. We also provided information about the needs of adult learners and generational differences within today's teaching force. This included practical applications of this knowledge. Then we shared models of how teachers develop over time as additional information that can be used to increase the self-knowledge of teacher leaders and help them in their work with other teachers. In the next chapter, we focus on more knowledge for teacher leaders related to understanding schools as organizations, change theory, and the importance of school culture and school climate to teacher leadership. Additional activities, readings, and scenarios, and questions for reflection and discussion are available in the companion website for this book.

CHAPTER 5

Additional Knowledge Needed by Teacher Leaders

Productive educational change roams somewhere between over-control and chaos. . . . You cannot mandate what matters, because what really matters for complex goals of change are skills, creative thinking, and committed action.

(Fullan, 2001)

VIEW FROM A SCHOOL LEADER	VIEW FROM A TEACHER LEADER
Mrs. Brown, I think you might feel more comfortable taking on some leadership roles if you could participate in some professional development experiences that would help you learn more about school policy and using systems thinking to address our school's culture. These are some of the topics the school leadership team wants to tackle this year.	*Mr. Peterson, that sounds pretty interesting to me, and I would also like to be involved in creating a better climate for parent involvement at our school. Is improving parent involvement on the agenda for the school improvement team this year? Maybe I could find out what other schools are doing and share that information with the school improvement team?*

This chapter focuses on additional knowledge needed by teacher leaders that includes understanding educational policy, systems thinking, schools as organizations, change theory, and the importance of school culture and school climate. This includes what teacher leaders need to understand about how educational policies are made, how thinking from a systems theory perspective can help teachers become better leaders, and how teachers can advocate within the systems that affect them. We also address why parent involvement that is culturally responsive is important knowledge for teacher leaders. Knowing how to conduct teacher action research is also key to developing as a teacher and teacher leader, so this inquiry-based process is introduced as a way to gain additional knowledge. However, we describe how to conduct teacher action research in great detail in Appendix B. Specific questions answered in this chapter include:

1. Why is educational policy and systems thinking important knowledge for teacher leaders?

2. How does change theory and organizational theory influence your work as a teacher leader?

3. How can teacher leaders influence school culture and school climate?

4. What constitutes effective parent involvement that is culturally responsive?

5. Why can teacher action research be used to increase the knowledge base for teacher leadership?

WHY IS UNDERSTANDING EDUCATIONAL POLICY AND SYSTEMS THINKING IMPORTANT KNOWLEDGE FOR TEACHER LEADERS?

Schools and districts are organizational systems embedded in larger complex systems made up of many interacting, interrelated, and interdependent components that interact with and affect other parts of the system. Most teacher preparation programs do not encourage their teacher candidates to understand education using a systems-thinking approach. However, once teachers become embedded in their schools, they find themselves responding to local, state, and national policies. Teacher leaders are embedded in multiple systems, whether they stop to think about this or not. Therefore, we think that systems thinking is important for teacher leaders to understand (Davis & Sumara, 2006; Senge et al., 2000). Adoption of systems thinking means that teacher leaders understand they are more than just one component in their school; rather, they are part of a system embedded in other systems such as districts and state systems of education. Therefore, it is important for teacher leaders to know how their school context, the culture and history of the surrounding community, and both the economic and political environment influence local, state, and national educational systems, and vice versa.

In other words, taking a systems-thinking approach means understanding that all parts of the system have to be considered in concert when trying to innovate or change. It also means acknowledging that adding or changing any part of a system will disturb other parts of the system, although usually not enough to make a real difference in the entire system. The times, culture, policies, economics, and politics all affect our educational systems. Not appreciating the complexity, and sometimes chaotic and random nature, of a system may lead to frustration. Ultimately, we believe that taking a systems-thinking approach will help teacher leaders better understand the complexity of schools and districts and better understand their roles and responsibilities within those systems. Basically, taking a systems-thinking approach means understanding that change is complex and affected by many things simultaneously. It also means understanding that we all have to work together.

All parts of the system have to be considered in concert when trying to innovate or change.

As we mentioned above, not many teacher preparation programs teach systems thinking or address educational policymaking. Other than learning about major policies such as No Child Left Behind, or its successor known as the Every Student Succeeds Act (ESSA), teacher candidates typically do not learn much about educational policymaking. They do learn about Title I schools and understand that they have policies for providing Free and Reduced Price meals for students who live in poverty. They also learn about Response to Intervention (RtI) and the Common Core State Standards (CCSS). However, often they do not know how, why, or by whom these policies were developed or how they are tied to economics and politics.

Education today is driven by mandates and policies. Educational policies, no matter their source, influence the responsibilities, and sometimes prescribe the actions, of teachers and teacher leaders. Many instructional and intervention strategies, assessments, curricula, and other mandates began as local, state, or national policies or are the result of such policies. Teachers know about policies for working with students with disabilities, such as the Individuals with Disabilities Act (IDEA), and related responsibilities and strategies for assessing and providing interventions for students with identified disabilities and/or for students with below grade-level achievement. However, what sometimes seems to be a policy is really something else. For example, RtI is an intervention strategy, although it has become a policy in many districts and states. Other mandates adopted by states, such as the CCSS, are really a set of standards that have become curriculum and policy mandates in many states. Mandated student assessments, including the use of the outcomes of these assessments to evaluate teachers, have become policies that greatly impact every educator, even though most teachers had no say in creating them. Furthermore, some of these assessments were never intended to be used to assess teacher performance.

Many educational policies are made at the local level by elected school boards and carried out by school principals under the direction of the central administration. Superintendents often propose local policies, but school board members also initiate policies, and it is the school board that ratifies local and state policies. However, local control of schools has waned in recent years because districts are influenced, and sometimes constrained by, state and national policies imposed on them by elected legislators at the state level or by elected members of Congress. State and national policies are influenced by the U.S. Department of Education as well as by other agencies and organizations that fund research and propose policies. In recent years, several states competed for Race to the Top funds from the federal government and in return promised to implement new policies to evaluate students and rate teachers and schools, for example.

School, district, and state policies are constrained by how they are funded, and funding is influenced by the health of the economy, as well as by politics. Furthermore, state and federal lawmakers are influenced by voters, lobbyists, including by lobbyists from teachers' unions such as the National Education Association and American Federation of Teachers, as well as by the U.S. Department of Education and the president. Lawmakers at the state and federal level are influenced by their staff, whose job it is to develop policies. Many legislative staff members typically represent political parties and special interests. In addition, political campaign donors also influence educational policy, as do the results of research and evaluation of grants and other education initiatives. In other words, education today is a complex political system affected by many different perspectives and special interests.

As you can see, the system surrounding educational policymaking has many interrelated and interdependent components all interacting to create policies that directly influence teachers, teacher leaders, and schools. Knowing that policies can originate at several levels is knowledge teacher leaders need to understand the system so they can become advocates at the appropriate level. At the very least, teacher leaders should always use their right to vote as citizens to advocate for their interests, but there are other ways to advocate as well.

Clearly, we think that teacher leaders need to understand the following: what educational policy is and is not; how policies are made; teachers' rights and responsibilities regarding local, state, and national policies; and how they can influence educational policy both locally and at the state and national levels. One way we offer this knowledge is by asking a person with local or state policy experience to speak to the teacher leaders we work with because we are not the experts in the policy arena. Alternatively, we recruit teachers who are active in either a local teachers' union or another teacher advocacy group. State Teachers of the Year (TOYs) make wonderful guest speakers who can talk about policy and advocacy, as do faculty or graduate students from a nearby college or university who study educational policy. School board members also make excellent guest speakers who can talk from experience about educational policies. These people can help teacher leaders better understand educational policymaking, as will the activity described next. Additional skills needed to become advocates who can reach out to affect educational policies at the local, state, and national levels are discussed further in Chapter 7.

ACTIVITY: In support of better understanding educational policy, engage whole-heartedly in one or both of the following activities:

A.   Look for current information about educational policy: in the news (such as on National Public Radio), newspapers (online or paper-based), online blogs, websites of various professional organizations (including the National Education Association), union websites, Twitter, or in any other online sites that report on or discuss and debate educational issues. Locate a news item about educational policy to discuss with other teacher leaders.

B.   When the state legislature is in session, find out what new policies legislators are proposing related to education as well as specific committees that address educational issues. Most state legislatures have a searchable database. Choose an issue or policy that interests you and then locate secondary sources related to this policy. Then compare the actual proposed legislation (primary source) to what various constituent groups are saying in support of or against the particular policy (secondary sources) being considered by the legislature. When the legislature is not in session, you can go to the U.S. Department of Education website and to the websites for the U.S. House of Representatives or the U.S. Senate to see what policies are being considered, and then to various secondary sources for a variety of opinions.

HOW DOES UNDERSTANDING CHANGE THEORY AND ORGANIZATIONAL THEORY INFLUENCE YOUR WORK AS A TEACHER LEADER?

In addition to understanding educational policymaking and systems thinking, teacher leaders also need to know something about organizational theory because they work in schools, which are organizational systems. They also need to understand change theory because it will help them understand how to work with teachers more effectively when a new policy, curriculum, assessment, or other mandate is imposed—whether it is an internally or an externally generated change.

Organizational theory. Schools are organizations with particular kinds of structures and specialized relationships among the people who work in them. All schools use a similar process, teaching, to achieve similar goals, such as student achievement. However, as with any organization there may be conflict about how to achieve established goals for any number of reasons because schools are embedded in multiple systems that are influenced by their culture as well as by policies, economics, and politics. Teacher leaders are one part of the organization that is school, and therefore need to know some things about organizational theory to understand more about how schools as organizations may be successful or unsuccessful, functional or dysfunctional.

Teacher leaders also need to be cognizant about how both the formal and informal systems operate in their school, including what the hidden curriculum is in their particular context. Snyder (1971) defined the hidden curriculum as a system of "implicit demands (as opposed to the explicit obligations of the visible curriculum) that are found in every learning institution and which students have to find out and respond to in order to survive within it" (p. 6). By curriculum, however, we are not talking strictly about the content students must learn, but more broadly and figuratively about how things operate in particular classrooms and schools and what needs to be learned to be successful in a particular organizational system. For teacher leaders understanding the hidden curriculum includes knowing the implicit messages communicated in their workplace and how power relationships operate in their schools and also in the other systems in which schools are embedded. With some knowledge about schools as organizations, we think teacher leaders will be more successful operating in their school's organizational system so they can help improve things for everyone involved—students, teachers, staff, parents, families, and so on.

Brandt (1998) wrote that "[s]chools can be learning organizations . . . by (1) creating conditions that support the learning of individual staff members, and (2) realigning the structure and processes of the entire organization to support continuous adaptation and change" (pp. 52–53), especially when they have achievable and shared visions and goals.

In addition, organizational theory tells us that organizations develop, grow, and change over time (Brandt, 1998; Senge et al., 2000) and that the parts that make up organizations (e.g., departments, teams, grade levels, administration, etc.) might be tightly coupled (unified, connected, dependent, coordinated) or loosely coupled (disconnected, separated, independent, uncoordinated) (Orton & Weick, 1990; Weick, 1976). Typically, parts of organizations that are tightly coupled function well together, are more standardized, and react to change in a consistent manner; whereas loosely coupled organizations are characterized by allowing many ways to achieve an end, may be less well organized, and may resist change. However, they also may be more sensitive and ready to adapt to change (Weick, 1976). In today's standards-based era in education, the trend is for the systems to be more tightly coupled, partly because they are more efficient and things get done in a consistent manner. The extent to which this occurs in the context in which teacher leaders are working, including at the school, district, and state level, is important to understand. In sum, knowing whether the parts of your school as an organization are more loosely or more tightly coupled may explain how well your school can adapt to change and survive disruptions or uncertainties caused by new leadership, policies, curriculum, assessments, or other mandates.

Further, in the life cycle of organizations, sometimes organizations are stagnant and not growing, sometimes they are active and in the process of learning to do new or different things, sometimes they are on an upswing and improving, and sometimes they are dysfunctional or even failing. In discussing the stages of development of an organization, Brandt (1998) stated,

> Members of a learning organization are aware that their institution does not arrive at its final destination instantly and must develop one step at a time. They have a clear sense of what they're trying to do, what progress they have made, and what still needs to be done. (p. 63)

In all cases, it is important for teacher leaders to think about their school as an organizational system and to evaluate where things stand with regard to overall organizational life history in general and with regard to teacher leadership more specifically. The following activity is one way for teacher leaders to begin to think about their schools as organizational systems.

ACTIVITY: Thinking like an ethnographer who studies cultures, make a study of your school as an organizational culture. Think about how you would describe the underlying norms, values, beliefs, traditions, and rituals that go into making up the culture of your school. Now write about how things are done currently at your school. Think about how people communicate and interact and what the explicit and implicit rules and ways of being are. Write about how your school is structured and how things get done, or not, at your school. How closely do people and departments or teams work with one another? How tightly connected are the teachers, staff, and administrators? Would you consider your school to be a tightly or loosely coupled organization? Once you have written your initial thoughts, do some observing, listening, and interviewing to learn more about your school as an organization. Pay attention to how things do and do not happen and who holds the power to make things happen or not. Try to uncover what you think might be the "hidden curriculum" at your school. What is expected of students, teachers, other staff, administrators, parents, and so on? What are the unwritten "rules"? Finally, revise and expand your initial writing based on new insights you gain from observing, listening, and talking to others. Share your revised interpretation of your school as a learning organization with some trusted peers to see if they agree or have different interpretations. Continue to revise your insights so that you are as conscious and aware of how your school's culture and how your school operates as an organization so that you can be prepared to work within it—or help change it, if need be.

Because schools as organizations are always changing—especially when there is a new principal, new staff, when curriculum textbooks change, when we are asked to use new assessments or new technology, or some other policy mandate is handed down—we also believe that it is important for teacher leaders to know about how change works.

Change theory. One useful explanation of how change affects people is the Concerns-Based Adoption Model (CBAM). Originally developed by Hord, Rutherford, Huling-Austin, & Hall (1987), this theory explains the process of change and how people respond to change by describing the types of questions they ask and the concerns they articulate. In sum, CBAM is a process-oriented approach that can reveal individual reactions to change, especially in educational contexts. For almost 30 years, CBAM has provided information and guidance to professional developers and other school leaders as they begin to think about introducing changes. We believe this model is useful for teacher leaders to know about and use when participating in and leading change efforts in their schools. For example, knowing about people's levels of concern can be helpful to teacher leaders when they plan professional learning opportunities, used when explaining changes to parents and families, and used with new teachers they might mentor. Such knowledge is both personally and professionally useful.

Teachers' comments and questions reveal their stages of concern. For example, early in the change process teachers may ask questions to gauge what a new policy, curriculum, assessment, or other mandate is all about. When teacher leaders hear questions such as "What is this all about?" or when teachers make statements like "I don't know what this is," or "I don't understand this," they need to be provided with clear definitions and detailed explanations of how things will work including specific information about what changes teachers should expect. Other questions that come early in the process of adapting to a change may be more about the "self" with educators asking, "What is in it for me?" "Why do I need to change?" When teacher leaders hear these kinds of questions they need to be ready to address how the change(s) will personally affect teachers, what the plan is for making the change(s), and how much time it will likely entail. As the change process proceeds, questions and concerns will be focused more on activities required by the change and how they can fit into teachers' other duties. At this time, when you hear questions such as "How am I going to do this?" or statements such as "I am spending all my time creating new materials for this," you must be ready to support teachers in managing change in a variety of ways. For example, teacher leaders might assist other teachers by both acknowledging their efforts and asking peers to share resources.

Later in the change process, teachers may focus more on the impact a change is having on their students and be concerned if change(s) they are trying to make are working. Even later teachers facing change may wonder how others are responding to the change(s) and if there is more to learn by sharing with others who are also working to change. When teacher leaders hear other teachers asking "Is this working?" or "How can I improve what I am doing to have more impact?" they need to increase opportunities for teachers to share what they are doing with others and learn about what others are doing locally and in other places. Teacher leaders basically need to keep the lines of communication open among those involved in the change. Throughout the process of adapting to change, it is important for teacher leaders to both understand and acknowledge the concerns and questions others have. Table 5.1 describes each level of concern teachers might have about a change, how they may express that concern in general, and how they might express concerns about a new curriculum mandate as an example. In this case, we use statements we heard teacher leaders express about the CCSS when they were replacing the traditional curriculum in North Carolina.

TABLE 5.1 Stages of Concern—The Concerns-Based Adoption Model (CBAM)

STAGES OF CONCERN	GENERIC EXPRESSIONS OF CONCERN	QUESTIONS/CONCERNS ABOUT CRITICAL CULTURAL COMPETENCE
Level 0—Bringing Awareness	I don't know anything about it (i.e., the Common Core).	What is this new curriculum? I don't see a need to change my current curriculum.
Level 1—Gathering Information	What is it? What is this all about?	What is the Common Core all about? How is it the same or different from our current curriculum?
Level 2—Making It Personal	How will it affect me?	How will changing to the Common Core affect me as an educator? Will I have to become a different kind of educator?
Level 3—Managing It All	How am I going to become skillful at this? How am I going to be able to manage my time to do this?	How will I find the time to apply the ideas from the Common Core to my teaching? It is taking too much time to adapt my instruction with this new curriculum.
Level 4—Realizing Potential Benefits and Consequences	How is this impacting my learners? How can I refine my skills to have more impact?	Are my students doing better because of my efforts to use the Common Core standards? What else can I do to be better at using the Common Core?
Level 5—Collaborating With Others	How are others doing with this? How can I connect with others doing the same things?	Can I share what I am learning about my students as I adapt to using this new curriculum? How are other teachers adapting to this new curriculum?
Level 6—Refocusing and Reenergizing	I have some insights I would like to share with others. I have some additional questions I would like to explore.	How can I share additional information and insights about what is working for my students? I think other educators need to know what I have learned about the Common Core.

SOURCE: Modified from Hord et al. (1987). *Taking charge of change*. Alexandria, VA: ASCD.

Change is a process that often provokes anxiety, which is NORMAL. Change is also inevitable in education. When confronting change, teachers need to be flexible, open, and willing to ask for help. Teacher leaders not only need to model these dispositions, but also know that it is important to celebrate successes along the way and stay open to leading during change(s) because they understand the process of change. The tips provided in Table 5.2 are useful for leading others through their concerns about change.

TABLE 5.2 Tips for Dealing With Change

- Learn from previous experiences—you have met change before and survived
- Realize that others can help—that you are not alone
- Understand that change is not out to get you—although it might seem that way at times
- Conduct yourself in a thoughtful and caring way during stressful times
- Realize that you cannot control all of the elements in life
- Learn that humility is an asset and bonus during times of change
- Do not forget your value system during the change process
- Know that if others can do something then so can you
- Accept the inevitable without a big fight—reserve your energies
- Understand that you are not fragile and will not break at the first sign of change

> *Leading in a culture of change means creating a culture (not just a structure) of change. —Michael Fullan*

Michael Fullan (2001) said,

Leading in a culture of change means creating a culture (not just a structure) of change. It does not mean adopting innovations, one after the other; it does mean producing the capacity to seek, critically assess, and selectively incorporate new ideas and practices—all the time, inside the organization as well as outside it. (p. 44)

Also, we know that it is important for teachers to consider the context in which change occurs. This includes understanding the current times and the political context, but locally it includes knowing what one's school culture and school climate are all about and how these things influence what teacher leaders can do.

HOW CAN TEACHER LEADERS INFLUENCE SCHOOL CULTURE AND SCHOOL CLIMATE?

Because school culture, school climate, and leadership are central to improving schools (Dawson & Rakes, 2003; Deal & Peterson, 2009; Fullan, 2001), there are several reasons for teacher leaders to understand their school's culture and climate so that they can influence it through their leadership. First, we know that successful teacher leadership depends on the culture of a school as well as the support of the school leader(s) (Angelle, 2007; Katzenmeyer & Moller, 2009). Second, MacNeil, Prater, and Busch (2009) found that school culture and school climate are influenced by a school's leadership, but that school culture also mediated what school leaders were able to accomplish by either supporting or limiting what they are able to do by themselves. Third, MacNeil et al. (2009) also found that when schools fail to address the importance of culture and climate, they fail to improve their students' achievement. In fact, organizational culture is important to understand because having focused goals and being adaptable are two factors that are crucial to the academic success of schools (MacNeil et al., 2009). Fourth, if changes are made to a school's organization without addressing the school's culture, those changes do not usually take hold (Fullan, 2001; MacNeil et al., 2009). For these reasons, understanding school culture and school climate is important knowledge for teacher leaders.

As described by MacNeil et al. (2009), norms, values, attitudes, expectations, rituals, behaviors and climate are all aspects of school culture, while others have "described school climate as the heart and soul of the school and the essence of the school that draws teachers and students to love the school and to want to be a part of it" (p. 75). School culture is mainly about shared norms and the ways things are done at a particular school, and school climate is about shared perceptions. Also, researchers typically operationalize school climate by studying the physical and structural environment of schools, job satisfaction, and relationships between teachers and leaders (MacNeil et al., 2009). Therefore, school culture and school climate are close cousins, and the differences between school climate and school culture are mainly about how these constructs are measured.

It is easy to see why *school culture* and *school climate* are often used interchangeably, but we agree with Van Houtte and Van Maele (2011) that school climate is one aspect of school culture. Further, we think it is not as important for teacher leaders to know the distinctions as it is for them to know what their school's culture and climate is and understand how it affects them and others in their setting. Given that these definitions overlap in both research and practice, we use the term *school culture* in the remainder of this chapter to discuss how teacher leaders can influence their school. According to Brown (2004), you want a school culture that includes

1. An inspiring vision, backed by a clear, limited and challenging mission

2. A curriculum, modes of instruction, assessments, and learning opportunities that are clearly linked to the vision and mission and tailored to the needs and interests of the students

3. Sufficient time for teachers and students to do their work well

4. A pervasive focus on student and teacher learning, coupled with a continual, schoolwide conversation about the quality of everyone's work

5. Close, supportive teacher-student, teacher-teacher and student-student relationships

6. Many opportunities and venues for creating culture, discussing fundamental values, taking responsibility, coming together as a community and celebrating individual and group success

7. Leadership that encourages and protects trust, on-the-job learning, flexibility, risk-taking, innovation and adaptation to change

8. Data-driven decision-making systems that draw on timely, accurate, qualitative and quantitative information about progress toward the vision and sophisticated knowledge about organizational change

9. Unwavering support from parents

10. District flexibility and support for multiple school designs, visions, missions and innovations. (p. 4)

ACTIVITY: In Appendix A you will find a survey titled *School Culture Review* based on key elements from the literature that influence school culture (Roby, 2011). Complete and score this survey to assess your school's culture. Considering each of the questions posed offers you an opportunity to assess the current norms of your workplace and the capacity for shared leadership. Scores are explained regarding the relative health of your school's culture, especially with regard to its support for teacher leadership. A deeper look into the five questions with the highest and lowest scores will provide you with insight about specific strengths and areas that may need to be improved. Completing this survey as an individual is worthwhile, but asking others in your school to complete this survey and comparing their results with yours is even more useful. School leaders should also complete this survey and compare their results with others, so encourage them to do this.

WHAT CONSTITUTES EFFECTIVE PARENT INVOLVEMENT THAT IS CULTURALLY RESPONSIVE?

One important aspect of school culture is how parents and families are involved, how they are perceived, what roles they can play, and what access or influence they feel they have. As educators we need to know about our students' backgrounds and how they learn, whether or not we are new or experienced teachers, and whether or not we are advocates for parent involvement. We need to know how to work with all kinds of parents and families and see parents and families as a resource to help us teach our students. Therefore, it is useful for teacher leaders to think honestly and thoughtfully about *how* we are engaging with parents and *why* we are doing so (or not). As teacher leaders, we need to develop a deeper, more sophisticated knowledge base about parent involvement.

Parent involvement is linked to both the social and academic achievement of students; in fact, researchers have suggested "the missing link in educational equity, in terms of achievement, is parental involvement" (Larocque, Kleiman, & Darling,

2011, p. 115). Furthermore, Henderson and Mapp (2002) described numerous benefits for students when their families are involved in their education:

> (1) higher grades and test scores; (2) higher rates of homework completion; (3) enrollment in higher level classes; (4) promotion, passing classes, and earning college credits during high school; (5) attending school regularly; (6) demonstrating better social skills; (7) showing improved behavior; (8) having positive attitudes about and liking to go to school; and (9) graduating and moving to postsecondary education." (as cited in Cooper, He, & Levin, 2011, p. 119)

For these reasons alone, teacher leaders need to be concerned about parent involvement in their schools.

Every teacher and leader knows that reaching out to and involving parents is important to the success of their students, but they may not always know how to reach all parents and families effectively, or why some efforts don't work as well as others. Often there are sociopolitical, generational, linguistic, and cultural barriers that exist between today's teachers who are mainly female, white, middle class, and monolingual compared to the increasing number of ethnically and linguistically diverse students and families in today's schools. Some educators consider culturally and linguistically diverse students and their families deficient because they may not be as fluent in Standard English and are therefore considered a "problem" when it comes to communication. Culturally and linguistically diverse families may be perceived as lacking resources—knowledge, experiences, and education—to help their children succeed in school. Sadly, some educators think that lack of parental involvement is indicative of a lack of parental interest (Arias & Morillo-Campbell, 2008). This reveals a deficit perspective, which leads to blaming the family rather than the school as a system that is not functioning well for the families of its children. Changing or eliminating deficit perspectives can change the ways families interact with schools.

We need to know how to work with all kinds of parents and families and see parents and families as a resource to help us teach our students.

Differences in cultural expectations can lead to misunderstandings about expectations for parental/family involvement in schools. Therefore, parent involvement must go beyond just trying to establish one-way, or even two-way, communication with parents/families. Parents/families are quite interested in their children's education, even if they do not participate in traditional ways that schools find acceptable. For example, some parents' work schedules or lack of transportation do not allow them to come to school during the day to volunteer or attend events, or to attend school conferences or meetings at night. Some parents/families may not be as well versed enough in the academic content their children are learning to assist them. As a result, when homework is not completed, some teachers become frustrated and blame parents and families for not caring for or about their children.

For all these reasons, as Cooper (2009) stated we need to "reframe the discourse on parent involvement so it is more contextualized, inclusive, culturally sensitive, and critically informed" (p. 390).

Auerbach (2007) suggested, "Traditional parent involvement models of family-school partnerships offer little insight into questions of access for marginalized populations" (p. 251) because "parent roles in education and the home-school relations in which they are embedded are a reflection of broader social inequalities that affect students" (p. 251). For these reasons it is important for teacher leaders to know about culturally responsive practices for parental involvement. They should not only know about traditional ways to involve parents (e.g., Epstein, 2001, 2002) but also learn about and use more culturally responsive models of parent and family involvement (Arias & Morillo-Campbell, 2008; Cooper, 2009; Cooper et al., 2011) to take a leadership role in effectively involving parents and families in their school. This includes using a systems-thinking approach to help others better understand and navigate the complexity of beliefs, values, and perspectives of parents and educators to increase the learning outcomes for all students.

Ultimately, we think this requires thinking about parent and family involvement as a social justice issue because social justice is about working to dismantle systems and power structures that marginalize some groups and privileges others. Using a social justice lens to look at parental/family involvement does not mean focusing on inadequacies. Instead it means building meaningful relationships with parents and families, meeting them where they are, and both advocating for and working with parents and families in more culturally responsive ways. Increasing parent efficacy will positively impact students' academic and social success (Cooper, 2009), which is the same goal teachers have. It also means becoming an agent of change and empowering others to do the same, which is leadership. With appropriate knowledge, teacher leaders can help implement practices and policies to include low-income and ethnically diverse parents in decision-making processes involving parents and families in schools, which equates to parent empowerment.

Epstein (1995) suggested that schools could help parents participate in their children's education in several ways. She proposed a developmental framework with six types of parent involvement (Epstein, 2001) that is used to guide parent involvement in many schools. We summarize this traditional model in Table 5.3.

Although Epstein's six-part model for parental involvement promotes the integration of home, school, and community to influence children's learning and development, it has been criticized as being "too school-based and Eurocentric" (Smith & Wohlstetter, 2009, p. 5). Given the composition and needs of today's more diverse families, nontraditional ways of parent and family involvement need to be considered. Moll and Greenberg (1990), for example, described the value of using students' funds of knowledge, which are the rich repositories of knowledge found in children's homes and communities, as a source for learning about how to best

TABLE 5.3 Traditional Model of Parent Involvement

TYPES OF INVOLVEMENT	DESCRIPTION OF TRADITIONAL PARENT INVOLVEMENT
Type 1—Parenting	Help all families establish home environments to support children as students.
Type 2—Communicating	Design effective forms of school-to-home and home-to-school communications about school programs and children's progress.
Type 3—Volunteering	Recruit and organize parent help and support.
Type 4—Learning at Home	Provide information and ideas to families about how to help students at home with homework and other curriculum-related activities, decisions, and planning.
Type 5—Decision Making	Include parents in school decisions, developing parent leaders and representatives.
Type 6—Collaborating With Community	Identify and integrate resources and services from the community to strengthen school programs, family practices, and student learning and development.

SOURCE: Adapted from Epstein (2001).

teach children from culturally and linguistically diverse families. Furthermore, regarding English language learners:

> Many ELL parents perceive their role as providing nurturing, teaching values and instilling good behaviors. They are often reluctant to take on responsibilities they traditionally view as being in the school's domain, regard teachers and schools as "the experts" and defer to them on tasks related to actual learning. (Arias & Morillo-Campbell, 2008, p. 10)

Therefore, a more culturally responsive model of family and parental involvement would operate in a shared, reciprocal fashion that is mutually beneficial to parents and to school personnel. Table 5.4 describes an updated model for parent involvement using the same six types as in Epstein's model. However, in Table 5.4 we offer descriptions of how parental involvement can be more culturally responsive.

Anderson and Minke (2007) found that parents of elementary students in an urban district in the Southwest indicated a great deal of involvement with their children in educational activities at home and also found that specific invitations from teachers had the largest effect on parent involvement. Therefore, teacher leaders need to be proactive in promoting and supporting parent and family involvement that is more culturally responsive. We have provided some information to help teacher leaders build their knowledge base in this area, but there is more to learn that parents, family members, and the community can teach. One way to do this is to talk with and learn directly from the elders and parents in their children's communities. Another way to do this is through teacher action research, which we introduce next and expand on in Appendix B. However, the best way to work with diverse parents and

TABLE 5.4   Culturally Responsive Model of Parent Involvement

TYPES OF INVOLVEMENT	DESCRIPTION OF CULTURALLY RESPONSIVE PARENT INVOLVEMENT
Type 1—Parenting	Make home visits to develop positive social relations with students and families and to provide teachers with insights to help make lessons more culturally relevant.
Type 2—Communicating	Use bilingual newsletters and multilingual homework hotlines to provide information and to support children's academic progress. Communication with parents and families can be improved by having home-school coordinators or bilingual liaisons to serve as information sources between schools and the families.
Type 3—Volunteering	Schedule events that accommodate families' work schedules, and provide child care to encourage attendance and participation. Instead of asking parents or other family members come to school for meetings or events, schedule meetings in the community. Provide options for parents to volunteer to assist teachers in ways that can be accomplished at home instead of at school.
Type 4—Learning at Home	Encourage and educate parents to get involved in homework and family literacy activities. Use interactive family homework activities that require students to interview or survey family members, use goods in the home to do math, read aloud to family members, write stories about family traditions and events, and learn to read and write in the family's native language, and so on. See Teachers Involve Parents in Schoolwork (TIPS) for ideas about interactive family homework at www.csos.jhu.edu/p2000/tips/subject.htm
Type 5—Decision Making	Teach parents about how the educational system works and strategies and skills that will empower parents and families to contribute to positive changes in schools (e.g., how to advocate for their children) and to hold schools accountable. Invite a diverse group of parents, or other family members, to serve on a parent advisory board.
Type 6—Collaborating With Community	Educators can learn a lot from visiting their school's community and interacting with parents, grandparents, pastors, shopkeepers, and public servants, and so on. This can help educators understand more about their students and garner support from the community. Diverse communities have many strengths, and these strengths must be recognized and incorporated into the curriculum.

families is to build strong relationships, listen and learn ways to build a welcoming school culture, and act in reciprocal ways that are mutually beneficial.

HOW CAN TEACHER ACTION RESEARCH BE USED TO INCREASE THE KNOWLEDGE BASE FOR TEACHER LEADERSHIP?

Action research has been defined as "systematic, intentional inquiry by teachers" (Lytle & Cochran-Smith, 1990, p. 83). Teacher action research yields knowledge that teacher leaders and other educators can gain about their professional practice by helping them understand and improve the nature and specifics of their practice. Teacher action research also helps teachers and teacher leaders develop a stronger voice when communicating about what they learn (Oberg & McCutcheon, 1987). Kemmis and McTaggert (1988) described action research as engaging in a cycle of questioning, planning, reflecting, acting, observing, reflecting, replanning, and often questioning further. This cyclical process sets teacher research apart from the regular problem solving that teachers do every day. We recommend teacher action research as a process for helping educators examine their practice critically and systematically. In Appendix B, we describe common steps for undertaking teacher action research that we hope teacher leaders will embrace. However, in the next few paragraphs we address why and how teacher action research increases the knowledge base for teacher leaders.

Baumann and Duffy-Hester (2001) emphasized teacher research as a metacognitive activity because "[i]t involves reflecting on one's teaching and practice, inquiring about it, exploring it, and then taking action to improve or alter it" (p. 78). We see this and many other reasons for teacher leaders to conduct teacher action research in their classrooms and schools. Some of the benefits we hear from teacher leaders we have mentored through their teacher action research projects include the following quotes. The knowledge they gained about themselves as teachers and teacher leaders, and about their students and fellow teachers, is invaluable.

I discovered throughout the project that being a researcher can open many opportunities in my classroom. I was able to evaluate my students, but more importantly myself. I listened to the audio recordings and paid close attention to the questions I was asking, how much time I allotted to let students think, if I interrupted them and other aspects of how I interacted with my students. By placing myself in a teacher researcher role I took a step back and looked at my classroom and the big picture I was trying to accomplish in math. I think in the future I will take this stance in more areas to improve my teaching and my students' academic understanding. . . . As a researcher, I was proud to have the opportunity to listen and reflect on this growth throughout the project. It makes me wonder what else I could improve in my classroom if I took a researcher point of view instead of just an educator one. (Amanda, 2015)

This research project has helped me grow professionally by allowing me to experience the challenges of implementing a professional development activity as involved as lesson study. It allowed me to see a different side of the teachers I work with and view my school beyond the walls of my classroom. . . . This project opened my eyes to the challenges of getting every teacher on board and moving in the same direction toward common goals. Every teacher that I spoke with about the project agreed that, as a school, we could use some help in adjusting to the new way of teaching aligned with the Common Core. We all agreed that a project like an adapted Japanese lesson study would be beneficial to us as a group, but when it came time to actually carry out the project, many teachers weren't as motivated as they first seemed. . . . As a teacher leader, I had to adjust to meet the needs of these teachers, which allowed me to grow professionally. . . . As far as future research goes, I really want to address the question of "What type or professional development for teachers best creates a paradigm shift that will move us away from procedurally taught mathematics and towards exploration and self-discovery of mathematics?" I believe lesson study is promising but would like to research other ways to better stimulate internal change in mathematics instruction beginning with teachers and hopefully permeating its way to the administrative top. (Will, 2013)

SUMMARY

In this chapter, we introduced the concept of systems thinking to address the complexity of prevailing forces in the development and use of educational policies, which are based on politics, economics, and laws. We also provided insight into the value of using change theory to understand the ways educational initiatives and policies may be taken up or resisted, and the importance of understanding all the interconnected nature of the educational "systems" currently in place. We also introduced ideas about organizational theory to assist both teacher leaders and their school leaders when implementing new programs or reforms successfully.

Change occurs regularly in the educational system; however, how we respond to change is influenced by school climate and school culture. In this chapter, we encouraged a deep review of the culture and environment in which your school operates. Finally, we looked at the need for teacher leaders to understand the nature of culturally responsive educational environments, especially focusing on the importance of building strong relationships with parents and families, learning from and with parents and community members, and involving parents and families as participants in decisions, activities, and curriculum. One way to accomplish these goals is to conduct teacher action research, which is a systematic investigation into practice and outcomes at the classroom or school level. Additional activities, readings, and scenarios are located in the companion website for this book, and Appendix B offers a detailed explanation of how to conduct teacher action research.

CHAPTER 6

Interpersonal Skills for Teacher Leaders

Whatever you do may seem insignificant, but it is most important that you do it.

—Gandhi

VIEW FROM A SCHOOL LEADER	VIEW FROM A TEACHER LEADER
Mrs. Brown, I know you have good time management skills already. I think that all the ways you use technology help you with that. You seem to be very tech savvy. Maybe you could use your online connections to help us gather information we need in our work on the school improvement committee. That would be a great contribution you could make as a teacher leader.	*Mr. Peterson, I know that not everyone is as comfortable as I am with digital tools, and I do have a lot of connections through my own PLN—my online personal learning network. In fact, I have been learning a lot about teacher leadership by reading blogs and asking for advice on Twitter. One thing I know I need to learn more about is conflict resolution. Does the school improvement team have a strategy for resolving conflicts?*

Teacher leaders often find themselves facilitating groups to develop a common agenda, agree on priorities, set goals, and turn the group's vision into reality. As teachers, they already use a lot of these skills with students, parents, and other professionals. However, as a teacher leader it never hurts to increase core interpersonal skills so they can be used metacognitively. Therefore, this chapter focuses on core interpersonal skills needed by teacher leaders: effective communication strategies, small- and large-group facilitation, time management, conflict resolution, and what we call digital efficacy, which includes being confident about knowing the right tool to use at the right time. Digital literacy, and a sense of efficacy about using digital resources to solve problems, support the interpersonal skills of communication and collaboration. All these skills are crucial for teacher leaders to master to be effective while working with others to develop a common direction and making the system work for the benefit of all. In addition, teacher leaders also need to be aware of the needs of all stakeholders so they can leverage everyone's contributions. Mastering the kinds of skills discussed in this chapter will help them accomplish this. Specific questions answered in this chapter include:

1. What effective communication strategies can teacher leaders use with various constituencies?

2. What skills can you use to facilitate groups successfully?

3. How do teacher leaders manage their time?

4. What digital tools will assist you as a teacher leader?

5. How can you use conflict resolution skillfully?

WHAT EFFECTIVE COMMUNICATION STRATEGIES CAN TEACHER LEADERS USE WITH VARIOUS CONSTITUENCIES?

In working with others, communication is key. Asking questions and listening carefully are critical interpersonal skills teacher leaders use all day long. Remembering to use active listening skills is key for teacher leaders—and worth teaching one's students to use as well. Active listening means that you

- show you are paying attention with your body language by leaning forward, keeping your eyes on the person speaking, nodding;
- verbally reflect back what you are hearing and learning;
- ask critical questions;
- create space for others to talk; and
- refrain from giving advice.

Active listening does require that you reflect on and repeat what you heard another person say, although for some people this may feel a bit contrived. Nevertheless, it is important to check for understanding and clarify what you think you heard. This can be accomplished by asking, *"What I think I heard you saying was . . . ? Is that correct?"* Teacher leaders especially need to use their active listening skills when leading small groups, including their professional learning communities (PLCs) and during other meetings, whenever dialogue is needed. Active listening also helps avoid misunderstanding and conflict.

As for asking questions, we suggest that teacher leaders use peer coaching language to enhance their interpersonal communication skills (Kurtts & Levin, 2000).

There are many coaching models (c.f., cognitive coaching, instructional coaching, peer coaching), but for our purposes we use peer coaching language that includes specific types of questions to ask for clarification, to elicit more information, and to make suggestions by asking leading questions. Giving specific feedback rather than general praise is also a part of using coaching language. Coaching language is particularly effective when teacher leaders are serving as mentors (Kurtts & Levin, 2000), but it is also very useful in any setting where dialogue is important, such as during parent conferences, PLCs, and in other meetings. More specifically, we teach teacher leaders to ask the following types of questions:

- **Clarifying questions** are needed when you do not understand something, or when there is a need to gather more information. For example, you might ask, "Can you please tell me why you decided to change the lunchroom procedures we were using?" or "Can you tell me how this new form will improve our referral procedures?"

- **Eliciting questions** are asked to prompt another person to explore alternatives or options and to say more or go deeper with the idea(s) being proposed or discussed. In other words, by asking this kind of question you are trying to elicit other possibilities. For example, you might ask, "Can you tell me more about why we are changing the lunchroom procedures?" or "What are some other ways you thought about doing referrals?"

- **Leading questions** are actually suggestions or recommendations for improvement that are turned into questions. Teacher leaders ask leading questions that imply another possibility or idea. However, they turn their suggestion into a question because it is better received than either stating an opinion or telling others what to do. For example, you might ask, "Did you consider having the students remain in the lunchroom until their teachers arrived?" or "What do you think about creating a new online referral form so we don't have to write the same information so many times?"

- **Praise is important** when using coaching language, but only when it includes concrete feedback. Consider the difference between saying to a colleague, "That's a great idea!" versus "That's a great idea because it is going to save everyone time and mean we won't be duplicating our efforts," or "I love the idea of having the students wait in the lunchroom because it means they won't be roaming the halls." The key word here is "because" since it affirms the idea suggested and reinforces the reasons why the suggestion is workable. Just saying "I love that idea!" is praise, but it stops short of highlighting and reinforcing the thinking behind the suggestion, which can be useful if there is a debate about how to solve the problem being discussed.

Debate vs. Dialogue vs. Deliberation. It is also important for teacher leaders to know how debate, dialogue, and deliberation are different and to promote and facilitate dialogue and deliberation whenever possible. *Debate* typically includes arguing the pros and cons of a topic. Debate is about trying to convince people that your argument is stronger or better.

> *Dialogue*, on the other hand, is about working together in a community of like-minded practitioners to understand our own belief systems that influence our work. The goal in a dialogue is to get to the bottom of an issue and then decide what to do about it. . . . The goal for our dialogue is not to decide which one way of thinking is the only right way. Rather, it is to build a common experience base that will allow everyone to learn together. (Qualters, 2010, p. 3)

Deliberation is a type of dialogue where the goal is to consider and weigh all sides of an issue before coming to a decision. Agreeing to compromise or taking a vote is often the result of careful, and sometimes protracted, deliberation. Table 6.1 includes guidelines for having a productive dialogue suggested by Qualters (2010).

TABLE 6.1   Guidelines for Productive Dialogue

Generative listening	Be aware of your own responses to the speaker. Does what someone else is saying make you glad? frustrated? nervous? If yes, say, "How can I clarify this? What else would you like to know?"
Suspension of assumptions	Identify and note an assumption when a participant makes it. Say, "Remember, we're here to identify your assumptions, find out why you believe them, and then find out if they're true." Or say, "Let's share ideas about (topic X) with each other and talk about it."
Active listening	Restate the speaker's statements before continuing the discussion. Say, "I am hearing you say_____. Is that correct?" Or say, "OK, now I hear you saying____. What do others believe?"
Observe the observer	Watch the group for their reactions. You might say, "I can see that many of us are having strong reactions to that statement. Let's discuss it further." or say, "Would someone whom I haven't heard from like to respond?"
Slow down the inquiry	Consider agreeing that after a statement is made, the group will silently let at least three seconds go by before anyone speaks. You might say, "Let's pause a minute to think about what we have heard."
Befriend polarization	Consider saying, "It looks like we have two different viewpoints. Let's hold off on any further discussion for a while; we'll sit with these different views and revisit them later."
Spirit of inquiry	You are there to inquire—not defend. Be open to what others say. You might say, "If you believe that's true, then let's talk about what makes that true."
Respect	This is the most important guideline. It encompasses all the other guidelines and the process itself. (p. 7).

Used with permission from Qualters, D. (2010). *A discussion guide for facilitators.* Madison, WI: Magna.

Each goal of the dialogue listed in the left-hand column is defined by questions teacher leaders can ask to keep a dialogue from turning into a debate.

ACTIVITY: Develop your own set of guidelines or norms for (a) the small groups you work with in workshops and classes you participate in with other teacher leaders; (b) your ideal guidelines for dialogue in the PLCs or committees you participate in or lead at your workplace; and (c) general guidelines for professional development sessions you lead now, or will likely lead. Once you have thought about the norms you think make for effective communication, take your ideas to your various constituent groups for deliberation. To get started, you can use the suggestions in Table 6.1 to develop a short list of guidelines for productive dialogue.

So far we have talked about important communication skills for teacher leaders, including active listening, asking questions using coaching language, the difference between feedback versus praise, and how dialogue and deliberation differ from debate. In addition, we find there are even more interpersonal skills teacher leaders need to be successful, which we address next.

I-messages. We believe that I-messages are also important for teacher leaders to exercise. I-messages help you communicate directly with another person by (1) describing the exact nature of the situation and (2) communicating your feelings and emotions clearly. Such communication can help prevent or relieve miscommunication and stress in a nonthreatening way because I-messages are focused on actions or deeds and not the person. For example, as a teacher leader you might need to say during a meeting, "I feel frustrated when everyone is talking at once because I cannot hear what each person is saying." Or when you are leading a professional development session you might need to say, "I am seeing a lot of heads down right now, which means to me that people are checking their phones. This concerns me because I fear you will miss some important information." I-messages are also useful in the classroom for communicating with students and are worth teaching students as a classroom management strategy. In this case, teaching and using the following simple sentence frame for stating I-messages helps.

---

1. Describe in a nonjudgmental, nonblaming manner what the specific behavior is perceived by you to be unacceptable.

   Example: *When I am interrupted when I am trying to give directions . . .*

2. State what tangible effect the behavior has on you.

   Example: *it disturbs my train of thought and I have to repeat everything, . . .*

3. State the feeling/emotion generated for you as a result of the specific behavior observed.

   Example: *and I get frustrated.*

Even if you do not think a full I-message is an appropriate response to a situation, at least describing a behavior and giving information about the effect the behavior has on you and others is a powerful way to communicate honestly. Furthermore, while I-messages are indirect, they can be followed by more direct requests. Using straight talk, redirecting, compromising, and using humor are also powerful communication strategies for teacher leaders. Restating your expectations is certainly appropriate. Using I-messages helps us acknowledge and take responsibility for our own feelings and emotions and helps us express feelings in a professional manner. I-messages are very useful for teacher leaders because they let others know the effect their actions and words have, but they put the focus on a behavior and not on a person. Of course, we recommend agreeing on ground rules or norms for any meeting rather than calling out people who are breaking "rules" they may not realize are unacceptable. This leads to talking about other skills needed for facilitating groups successfully.

WHAT SKILLS CAN YOU USE TO FACILITATE GROUPS SUCCESSFULLY?

Both working in a group and leading a group can be a great experience or a terrible one. Which way it goes depends to a large extent on the quality of the leadership in the group, communication among group members, planning for the needs of the group, and the respect people show for each other. As a teacher leader you may have or prefer to use a style that is either direct or nondirect. Teacher leaders with a directive style typically appear to be controlling because they assume that it is their responsibility to facilitate the group's process and keep the group on track. Direct leadership styles are useful in situations when a group needs to achieve a goal in a short time period; in such cases a more direct style of leadership might keep the group focused. Further, if a situation is particularly difficult, a directive leader might be needed to control the discussion and make sure that decisions are made in a timely manner.

Teacher leaders who have a less direct leadership style typically are perceived to be acting more like a facilitator. Facilitators who are nondirective try not to let their own agenda and preferences influence the group's deliberations—except when they need to ask questions or make statements that advance the work of the group. A good facilitator will help the group set rules for itself, make sure that no one dominates, and employ strategies to invite everyone to participate. Nondirective leaders encourage everyone to express their ideas and welcome ideas that may seem out of the box. Strong facilitators aim to keep deliberations open so that a conclusion is not reached too quickly or before everyone has been heard. For most group discussions, the facilitator role is probably a good one to use because it encourages respect for everyone's ideas, which leads to a more satisfying experience for each participant.

A good facilitator will help the group set rules for itself, make sure that no one dominates, and employ strategies to invite everyone to participate.

Table 6.2 contains some guidelines that teacher leaders can use to facilitate groups to work together successfully, although you may be able to think of others.

TABLE 6.2 Guidelines for Facilitating Successful Groups

Work hard	For all activities, do your share and a little bit more. Be responsible, and then add a little extra to bring the standards of the group up and make its success more likely.
Be inclusive	Bring every member of the group in on discussions, decision making, and activities. Give everyone a chance to speak, listen to them, and give serious consideration to what they are saying. Cooperate.
Take turns	Don't be the leader all the time. Don't be a follower all the time. Don't talk too much—listen to others. Don't just listen to others—share your opinions, too.
Be nice	Avoid personal criticism. Make sure you understand what someone is saying before you weigh in with your personal opinion. Give others the benefit of the doubt.
Be timely	Show up promptly for meetings. Meet all deadlines. When you are late, you waste people's time and make them mad. People depend on you. Get things done on time.
Don't be an enabler	If you have somebody who is not doing their work, hold them responsible as a group. Everyone needs to do their part.
Stay focused on the task	Make your meetings count. Do not drift into irrelevant subjects. Be mindful about what you need to accomplish.
Improve the mood of the group	Be positive. Be fun. Be appreciative of other people. Be full of good ideas. Do your part to make the environment a good one.
Don't cast blame unfairly	If there is a problem in the group, begin by asking what you have done (or not done) to contribute to that problem—and what you might do to fix it. If there is conflict, try to work it out through respectful dialogue with each other (not e-mail, a horrible conflict medium). Try to understand the other person's point of view as you discuss the issue.

Stages of Group Development. Group formation has been said to follow recognizable stages, known as "forming, storming, norming, and performing," although this may not be a strictly linear process. Psychologist Bruce W. Tuckman (1965) created this memorable phrase, and later added a fifth stage called "adjourning" or "mourning" (Tuckman & Jensen, 1977). We think it is important for teacher leaders to know how groups form and how they typically perform at each stage. Most groups appear to progress through a number of phases or stages as members get to know each other, develop some level of operating interdependently, and achieve goals in ways that are satisfactory to everyone. Groups also have to learn ways to deal with conflict.

We recommend that teacher leaders consider using Tuckman's model (Figure 6.1) to assess the groups they work with and to help their groups reach the performing stage as quickly as possible. In Tuckman's model, the role of the leader changes as the group develops from being more directive early in the process of forming and

FIGURE 6.1 Stages of Group Development

Forming

Team acquaints and establishes ground rules. Formalities are preserved and members are treated as strangers.

Storming

Members start to communicate their feelings but still view themselves as individuals rather than part of the team. They resist control by group leaders and show hostility.

Norming

People feel part of the team and realize that they can achieve work if they accept other viewpoints.

Performing

The team works in an open and trusting atmosphere where flexibility is the key and hierarchy is of little importance.

Adjourning

The team conducts an assessment of the year and implements a plan for transitioning roles and recognizing members' contributions.

SOURCE: http://wheatoncollege.edu/sail/leadership/student-involvement-handbook/strengthening-group/leadership-teambuilding/

storming to being more facilitative as group members get to know and trust each other during the norming and performing process. Teacher leaders can use various strategies to move groups through the stages of the group formation process. With focus and hard work, they can quickly develop high-performing teams. However, everyone must contribute and work to make the group epitomize a learning team. To help groups develop, teacher leaders can do the following:

1. Help the group to establish and monitor ground rules.

2. Remind group members of the importance of listening to each other.

3. Assist the group understanding that positive "conflict" is normal, and may even be a necessary part of group development.

4. Rotate the responsibility for group facilitation.

5. Be sure the purpose or mission of the group is clear to all and that the purpose/mission is revisited periodically.

6. Publicly recognize the contributions of group members.

7. Wrap up each session with meaningful and constructive comments about the group's progress and process.

ACTIVITY: To learn more about your leadership styles and strengths, and to see how you can contribute to the groups you are either working with or are leading:

A. First, go online to find a short quiz by typing "true colors test" into any search engine. True Colors was developed by Don Lowry and is based on the work of Isabel Briggs-Myers, Katherine Briggs, and David Keirsey who also developed personality-type inventories that can help teacher leaders to learn more about themselves. The True Colors quiz will ask you to prioritize sets of words linked to a color: blue, orange, gold, or green. Each color is a metaphor for a set of personality traits. Although everyone has a mix of traits, if blue is your main color you are very people-oriented, orange means you are very action-oriented, gold means you are pragmatic and a planner, and green personality types are independent thinkers. Use the descriptors for each color type to consider the strengths that each color type brings to a group. Because no one color is better or worse than another, the True Colors self-assessment helps you see the benefits of different color types working together in groups.

B. Next, complete the Keirsey Temperament Sorter KTS-II developed by David Keirsey (www.keirsey.com) to help you recognize your strengths as a teacher leader. This is a 70-question personality assessment that yields four temperament types Keirsey calls the Guardians, Ideals, Artisans, and Rationals. Once you take this free, online assessment, you can read about each personality type and realize the importance of recognizing how every member of a group has different strengths to bring to the group. We also encourage you to ask members of the groups you work with to take one or more of these assessments. Discussing the results is a great way to help groups become more aware of their strengths, hence more effective.

Group Protocols. We also suggest that teacher leaders introduce and make use of a variety of protocols to assist groups as they work together. Protocols provide step-by-step guidelines that can be used to structure group conversations about student work, teaching ideas, areas of conflict, and so on. Protocols typically include a time limit for each person's turn to talk and explain clearly when it is time to present, time to listen, and time to give feedback. The value of using a protocol is that everyone in the group knows the format and guidelines and agrees to follow them. This makes the time spent in conversations about teaching and learning more productive and focused, and therefore worth the time spent. Teacher leaders can sharpen their facilitation skills by choosing and using appropriate protocols, such as the tuning protocol described next. However, there are numerous protocols that can be used for a variety of purposes, including for professional development, standard setting, and accountability (McDonald, Mohr, Dichter, & McDonald, 2013).

The Tuning Protocol (McDonald et al., 2013) and adaptations of it (Easton, 2002) are often used when educators look at student work together, or when it is important to gain feedback about a change in or new educational effort. Teacher leaders can use the Tuning Protocol as a problem-solving tool and as a way to ensure that all presenters/groups receive direct and respectful feedback about the problem(s) and solution(s) they present to the groups for dialogue or deliberation. Protocols also offer presenters time to reflect on feedback they receive. This process also helps the audience "tune up" their own thinking by listening to the diverse and candid views of others. It forces presenters or groups to describe and frame particular problems clearly and to offer possible solutions that bear on that problem. It orients colleagues to examine the problem presented and the suggested evidence from both warm and cool perspectives. Its versatility as a learning tool for educators depends on two design features: (1) the separation of the presentation and the response, and (2) the use of both warm and cool responses.

The Tuning Protocol has been used extensively by the Coalition for Essential Schools, the Annenberg Institute, and Harvard Project Zero to gather feedback on school reform proposals. In Table 6.3, we describe how we used this protocol

TABLE 6.3 Tuning Protocol

1. **Introduction.** Someone in the group is selected or volunteers to be the facilitator for each session. The facilitator reviews the protocol goals and norms, and goes over the steps of the protocol. The facilitator is also the timekeeper. (~5 minutes)

2. **Presentation.** The presenter(s) share ideas for a teacher action research project about instituting a writer's workshop across their grade level. The presenter(s) explain the rationale for this proposal and the plan for studying the effects it has on student writing. The presenter(s) also provide a draft of proposed goals, objectives, assignments, activities, and assessments to be used to collect data on the effectiveness of using a writer's workshop. The presenter(s) may also highlight particular questions or areas they would like the audience to address in their response. During this step the respondents may not speak. (~15 minutes)

   Note. If student work is the focus, then about 10-15 minutes should be inserted at this point in the protocol to be used for everyone to look carefully at the student work samples provided by the presenter(s).

3. **Clarifying Questions and Responses (warm and cool feedback).** Respondents ask clarifying questions and note their warm and cool reactions to what the presenter(s) said. Warm reactions emphasize the strengths of the ideas and particular approaches to addressing the problem. Cool reactions emphasize problematic aspects or concerns. Often cool reactions come in the form of clarifying, eliciting, or leading questions: "I am wondering why you chose to . . . ?" or "I am curious about your interpretation of X. Could you talk more about X?" During this step the presenter(s) may not speak. Presenter(s) are strongly encouraged to take notes during this time and to think about which responses to comment on and which to let pass. (~10 minutes)

4. **Presenter Reflection.** The presenter(s) use notes taken during the question and response segment to react to any responses they choose. A response is not meant to defend a position but to think and talk more about the ideas offered by the respondents. During this step the respondents may not speak. (~10 minutes)

5. **Conversation/Dialogue.** Presenters and respondents engage in open conversation. (~10 minutes)

6. **Debriefing.** Participants reflect on the process and explore ways to use the protocol in other situations. The facilitator may ask, "How did it feel to hear warm and cool feedback? How did it feel not to be able to respond immediately to feedback? How can you use this protocol in other contexts or learning situations?" (~5 minutes)

Adapted from McDonald et al., 2013.

for a discussion of a proposal for a teacher action research project. However, the Tuning Protocol is used most often to look at samples of student work and student data, or to discuss unit plans, proposed assessments, rubrics, homework policies, classroom management plans, or grade-level, department, or school policies (Easton, 2002).

Think-Pair-Share. We often use the simple cooperative learning strategy known as Think-Pair-Share when it appears that a group is not ready to talk about a topic. Posing a question or two and asking each person in the group to think about and/or write a response before they share their responses(s) with a partner allows each person time to reflect and a chance to share their thoughts before the floor is open to discussion or deliberation by the whole group. This means that everyone has the opportunity to be engaged with the topic at some point, even if they do not want to participate in a large group discussion. We think the strategy of Think-Pair-Share, or just having talking partners or shoulder partners, is useful not only when facilitating groups during meetings or professional development, but also for classroom teaching. However, there are still other skills teacher leaders need to develop and exercise, including ways to manage time—both their personal time and time spent working with others in a leadership capacity—because time is always a concern for teacher leaders.

HOW DO TEACHER LEADERS MANAGE THEIR TIME?

One of the biggest concerns we hear from current or potential teacher leaders is the issue of time. There is never enough time for everything that is asked of teachers, so many feel that taking on a leadership role is too much. Katzenmeyer and Moller (2009) suggested many great strategies for finding time for teacher leadership. We use their lists as a catalyst for discussing time-saving ideas that are realistic and will benefit their schools. Here are the top five time-saving ideas they recently told us would work best. However, we know there are many more ways to use time more wisely, to free up time, to find common time, to restructure time, and even to purchase time (Katzenmeyer & Moller, 2009) if teacher leaders are just asked.

1. Save time in staff meetings for discussions, deliberations, or professional development (PD) by using e-mail or text messaging for all announcements.

2. Use technology for required district or state-level PD to save travel time. This includes making use of video, video conferencing, and offering online PD that can be accessed at school or from home.

3. Teach all teachers the skills they need to lead their PLCs efficiently and effectively so that time is not wasted in these meetings.

4. Utilize administrators, other staff, or parent volunteers to create duty-free times for teachers during the day.

5. Find time for mentors to observe and support their mentees by adjusting the master schedule.

Planning for Meetings. Related to saving time, one skill we stress to teacher leaders is the importance of planning for meetings they lead. This makes sense to them not only because they are used to planning for their students, but also because they do not like attending meetings with no agenda, and they hate meetings that end up being gripe sessions. Teachers also want to know the purpose of meetings they have to attend and what is planned so they can be prepared. Therefore, teacher leaders need to make sure there is an agenda and a set time period for any session they lead. Whether your leadership style is more directive or nondirective, an agenda indicates forethought, preparation, and respect for other people's time. It is also important that teacher leaders engage others in helping set agendas. At the very least teacher leaders should ask for additional agenda items at the start of a meeting. Sending out minutes is also something that teacher leaders need to make sure happens, whether they do this themselves or enlist a colleague to help them. Fortunately, technology can assist teacher leaders with agendas, minutes, and more. We focus next on digital tools that can be used to save time and enhance communication and collaboration, because these are key skills teacher leaders need to develop.

WHAT DIGITAL TOOLS WILL ASSIST YOU AS A TEACHER LEADER?

As we mentioned above when talking about managing time, teacher leaders can use technology to save time when it comes to communicating and collaborating with others. There are a number of digital tools that provide many advantages to busy teachers, teacher leaders, and administrators. For example, Google provides a suite of free tools that are especially useful for teachers and teacher leaders because they can be used by multiple people at the same time, and because they make it easy to distribute, access, and store various kinds of documents. For example, using Google Docs makes it easy not only to collaborate on creating agendas and sharing minutes, but also on writing the school improvement plans, developing a new plan or policy, writing curriculum or lesson plans, or creating common assessments. Such tools can make grant writing a collaborative process. Google Forms allows teacher leaders to create quick surveys when they need to do a needs assessment before starting something or getting feedback on how things are going. Google Forms can be used to create invitations and to gather data. Using Google's calendar app also saves time setting up and inviting people to meetings. Google Hangouts can be used for meetings with people who are not on site, or for communicating with parents and families. And Google Slides (or Prezi, for example) can be used to create presentations collaboratively.

For other communication needs, it is important for teacher leaders to know not only what digital tools they want to use and for what purpose, but also what tools others will find useful on the receiving end. There are many possibilities for communication: blogs, websites, Facebook groups, Twitter, podcasts, e-mail, text messaging, and even automated phone calls. Teacher leaders do not have time to use all of these, so it is important to determine what purpose each serves and then choose the right digital tool for the right purpose—and the right tool for the right audience. This is digital efficacy. We think that e-mail, text messaging, and automated phone calls are most useful for sending messages and announcements that are brief and need to be broadcast quickly. For tech-savvy parents and older students, you could add Twitter or Instagram to this list. However, when the message is longer, something you want to keep for a while, something that should be available any time, and/or something that would be enhanced with photos, then blogs, websites, podcasts, and Facebook are better tools for these purposes. Twitter may fit here, too, although these messages have to be very brief (140 characters). And while there is nothing wrong with paper newsletters for those who are not tied to their technology devices, this is changing constantly—as are the digital tools themselves. In fact, probably one of the most important dispositions a teacher leader needs is to be open to learning and using new digital tools that really are time savers and not time sinkers.

Aside from using digital tools for communication and collaboration, there are many other digital tools, also known as Web 2.0 tools, that teacher leaders we know find useful for collaborating on presentations, developing curriculum, and sharing what is going on in their classrooms and schools. Most of these are free and easy to use. Among the current favorites we hear about are Pinterest and LiveBinders for collecting resources for teaching instructional units, and numerous digital storytelling tools for encouraging students to write and create products that show what they have learned. Among our current favorites are Voicethread, Little Bird Tales, TarHeel Reader, Story Jumper, and Story Bird. The teacher leaders we work with also like both using and creating videos, which their students also benefit from using. Although it might not be a time saver, video is certainly valuable for both communication and collaboration, and many of the teacher leaders we work with like to see and use videos examples in professional development sessions they both attend and lead. (See Table 7.3 for other useful technology tools.)

HOW CAN YOU USE CONFLICT RESOLUTION SKILLFULLY?

Working with others can lead to conflict because people have differing goals, values, feelings, motivations, perceptions, ideas, or desires. Good communications may prevent some conflicts, but conflict is inevitable at some point; therefore, teacher leaders need to be skilled in conflict resolution. For teacher leaders facing conflict, the goal should always be to try to repair or restore any breakdown in relationships because we know relationships are key to teacher leaders. Therefore, we review here some common reasons for conflict and a protocol for addressing conflict that teacher leaders can use. We also describe some of the activities we use and questions we ask when discussing ways to resolve conflict with teacher leaders. For example, we know the following about conflict, which we share with teacher leaders as a reminder about how important it is to keep simple disagreements from escalating.

Conflicts can occur . . .

- When the concerns of two people appear to be incompatible, or
- When there are differences in interests, needs, desires, values, or
- When there is a scarcity of resources (time, space, roles, materials, funds, etc.), or
- When there is a rivalry and one person tries to outdo another
- If there is a competitive atmosphere
- When the climate feels intolerant or mistrustful
- When poor communication leads to misunderstanding and misperceptions
- If emotions are expressed inappropriately
- If someone misuses their power
- When conflict resolution skills are lacking

Conflicts can escalate . . .

- When there are increased emotions such as anger or frustration, or
- When there is increased threat
- If more people get involved or choose sides
- If people were not friends before conflict
- If the people have no peacemaking skills

Another thing we know about conflict is that it probably will not go away by ignoring it or pretending things are not that bad. Even if you are willing to forgive and forget, other people may not. Knowing how you define conflict, what things you consider to be conflict, and how you personally react to conflict are important steps to take before choosing strategies that might work to address conflict. Some people may have had conflict resolution training, or have both successful and unsuccessful experiences with conflict they can share, which is very helpful. Nevertheless, we begin our discussion of conflicts and conflict resolution with these activities:

ACTIVITY: (a) First, think about how you handle conflict: What kinds of conflicts have you experienced both personally and professionally? How have you tried to resolve these conflicts? How would you rate your knowledge of strategies to conflict on a scale of 1-10 (if 1 = I know nothing and 10 = I am an expert)? (b) Second, think

---

EVERY TEACHER A LEADER   https://resources.corwin.com/everyteacheraleader

about and later talk with a partner about what you typically do when you are con-fronted with conflict: Do you fear conflict? Do you feel comfortable disagreeing with more experienced or knowledgeable others? Does conflict make your heart race? Do you face conflicts head on? Do you try to solve the problem that created the conflict? Do you try to avoid conflict at all costs? Do you enjoy a lively dispute? Do you try to redirect or calm the situation? (c) Reflect on and perhaps share with a peer how you would answer the following questions: What were you taught by your family about how to handle aggressive behavior and conflict? What did you do when adults around you were in conflict? How did your family express feelings of anger or hurt? Were you punished or encouraged to express your feelings of anger or hurt? (d) Think about examples of typical conflicts that arise in schools. Think about and later discuss: What do you do when a conflict arises with a parent? With a colleague? With an administrator? With a student? Try to consider others' perspectives when thinking about conflict.

After we define conflict and discuss why conflict occurs, how it escalates, and how we personally react to conflict, then we talk about ways conflict can be de-escalated. Generally speaking, conflict can be de-escalated

- If attention is focused on the problem and not the people.

- If the emotions or perceptions of threat decrease.

- If the people involved were friends before the conflict occurred.

- If the people involved know how to make peace and resolve conflicts or have someone to help them do this.

We also share several stances and strategies that can be taken to resolve conflicts, as described in Table 6. 4.

Finally, we review a typical protocol used for conflict resolution that teacher leaders can use themselves and also teach their students. A typical problem-solving proto-col for resolving conflicts starts with having each person describe the conflict and how they are feeling. Only one person should talk at a time throughout this proto-col, which is something the teacher leader should monitor. The next step is to ask each person to restate what they heard the other person say to show they under-stand that person's issue, feeling, and perspective. Next, each person should suggest what could be done to solve the conflict. Several options for reparation or restitu-tion may be needed before both parties find and agree to a solution to the conflict. Once this is achieved, everyone involved must agree to follow the agreed-upon resolution to the conflict. Apologies may or may not be a part of the resolution, but we think it is valuable for both adults and students to take ownership for their part in any conflict and to apologize for their actions. As we often say, "Where you sit is

TABLE 6.4 Strategies for Resolving Conflicts

Work to resolve conflicts:	Try to resolve conflicts using a problem solving approach:
• Listen first without comment or challenge • Make eye contact and nod to show you are listening—Try saying, *"Mmm-hmm," "Uh-huh,"* or *"Yes"* • Repeat what you heard—Try saying, *"OK. What I heard you saying is . . . "* • Ask for clarification—Try saying, *"I think you want us to try switching classes. Have I got that right?"*	• Describe the conflict • Avoid statements like *"I have always . . . "* or *"You have always done this to me . . . "* • Use I-statements to identify your own goals • Think about the other person's point of view • Brainstorm multiple "win-win" compromises
Use your emotional intelligence to resolve conflicts:	**Try using I-messages to resolve conflicts:**
• Recognize the symptoms of excessive feelings in yourself and others—*Raised voices, red face, clenched fists, furrowed brow, change of tone, rapid heartbeat, steam out of ears!* • Don't react to the emotional outbursts of others • Make I-statements to identify your feelings • Listen to the goals and feelings of the other people • Separate the "people" from the "problem"	• I-messages are about actions/deeds and not about the person, so they can help prevent or relieve conflicts. • I-messages help you communicate directly with another person by (1) describing the exact nature of the situation and (2) communicating your feeling/emotions. Example: • *When I get interrupted when I am trying to explain this idea, it disturbs my train of thought and I get frustrated.*

where you stand," so you need to understand that different people have different perspectives that may have led to conflict, and teacher leaders need to be able to appreciate other people's perspectives, and help others do the same.

When serving as a mediator, teacher leaders need to provide a safe space for the conflicting parties to talk and then ensure that all the steps in the protocol are followed. If a teacher leader is one of the parties in a conflict, we hope you can internalize this protocol well enough to follow these steps. However, it may require a cooling-off period and not starting a conflict resolution session until emotions are lowered. Nevertheless, we see conflict resolution as a skill that can be learned and practiced. Ultimately, teacher leaders need to exercise both assertiveness and cooperation to resolve conflicts. The goal is to find a win-win solution so that all parties to a conflict are satisfied. Compromise may occur if someone is willing to make accommodations, but avoiding conflict is not a good option. Therefore, teacher leaders need to develop their skills for resolving conflicts that will rise inevitably when people are working together in high-stakes environments like schools.

SUMMARY

This chapter focused on the interpersonal skills that teacher leaders need to use regularly to work effectively with the myriad personalities, goals, and needs that every educational unit has. We discussed effective communication skills, including active listening, using coaching language, making I-statements, and other appropriate ways to provide encouragement and support in groups. We described the differences between debate, deliberation, and dialogue. We provided an overview of skills needed for facilitating small and large groups to accomplish both very specific and more theoretical types of goals. We also discussed the importance of effective time management given that every teacher is extremely busy. This chapter also included an overview of using digital tools to collaborate and communicate with other educators (as well as parents and students). Finally, we discussed ways to identify and resolve conflicts through the development of conflict resolution skills as a habit of mind. Each of these skills is important as teacher leaders strive to work with other adults in a collaborative and fruitful manner. Additional activities and scenarios to discuss can be found in the companion website for this book.

CHAPTER 7

More Skills for Teacher Leaders

Leadership is the capacity to translate vision into reality.

—Warren Bennis

VIEW FROM A SCHOOL LEADER	VIEW FROM A TEACHER LEADER
Mrs. Brown, your questions make me think that the school improvement team probably needs to do a needs assessment before we set our goals for the year. I think you could help us do this, given your strong technology skills and the strengths I have seen you exhibit when analyzing and making use of data in your PLC. This would be a great contribution you could make as a teacher leader in this school.	*Mr. Peterson, I agree that doing a thorough needs assessment should be a top priority this year. I would certainly like to help with a needs assessment, but I really hope this can be a collaborative effort. I don't think any one person would even know all the questions to ask, so we need to get input from as many people as possible. Maybe we can use technology to help us with the needs assessment.*

This chapter focuses on additional skills needed by teacher leaders as they take on new roles and responsibilities. These might include participating in and leading various professional learning opportunities including book clubs, instructional coaching, curriculum writing, mentoring, presenting at conferences, study groups, teacher research groups, workshops, writing grants, and advocating for their students and fellow teachers, as well as for education as a profession. The first set of skills we address in this chapter, how to conduct a needs assessment, will be very useful for every project that a teacher leader might be considering: preparing for a professional development workshop; considering a new or revised curriculum; developing a new practice, policy, or strategy; or undertaking responsibility for a special project. With time being a scarce resource, conducting a needs assessment can actually save time because the data collected help you focus the scope of your efforts. This is truly a skill set teacher leaders need to develop, and it leads into the other skills discussed in this chapter: planning for professional development, grant writing, and engaging in advocacy and outreach. Specific questions answered in this chapter include

1. How do you conduct a needs assessment?

2. How do you plan, deliver, and evaluate professional learning activities?

3. What skills do you need for successful grant writing?

4. What skills are needed for effective advocacy and outreach?

5. How do you use data and reflective practice as a teacher leader?

HOW DO YOU CONDUCT A NEEDS ASSESSMENT?

A needs assessment is a systematic way to gather information, including hard and soft data, from a variety of sources to help you plan next steps. A needs assessment can be used to provide information about any one (or all) of these five categories: ideals, norms, minimums, desires, and expectations. For example, "The goal of a college education for all citizens who desire one (an ideal)" is certainly different from a "goal of ensuring basic reading skills for all children (a minimum)" (Gall, Gall, & Borg, 2003, p. 559). Similarly, asking every teacher to teach writing (an expectation) is different from asking every teacher to use the same rubric to score student writing (a norm). Good leadership includes figuring out what is working well and what areas are in need of improvement.

When conducting a needs assessment, it is important to gather information from all relevant stakeholder groups to help with "setting objectives for curriculum or program development" (Gall et al., 2003, p. 557). Stakeholders may include parents, teachers, staff, and others from the community, depending on your goals or the project. In the case of considering how to lead a desired innovation, a needs assessment will help you learn what people already know, what they need and/or want, and what they fear. Another purpose for talking with all relevant stakeholders is to identify what they consider to be important while determining what is needed. Data collected for most needs assessments should include various kinds of student data, including both formative and summative assessments, because student success is always our goal. For example, school attendance and discipline records may be useful data depending on the project being considered, planned, or evaluated.

Aside from learning what is needed, conducting a needs assessment can help teacher leaders gain allies, buy-in, and collaborators. It is also a good way to determine who may have an interest in and/or expertise related to the topic or project being considered because, as we all know, teacher leaders should never work alone.

Ultimately, conducting a needs assessment can help teacher leaders maintain relationships with colleagues and build trust among all relevant stakeholders because you have involved them in the process of planning and/or evaluation.

Occasionally, educators believe that a needs assessment is not necessary because they have heard their colleagues speak about the topic frequently. Or perhaps it seems useless to engage colleagues in a formal needs assessment activity using the kinds of data sources that we describe below. However, we believe it is always good to give individuals a chance to speak their minds, either publicly or privately through an anonymous survey (online or on paper), during a focus group, or by conducting individual interviews, even informal ones. In all cases, it is important to remember that just planning for and conducting a needs assessment is not enough. Gathering input has to be followed by analyzing the data collected and sharing it with others. Making both the goals and the results of your needs assessment transparent goes a long way toward making the time you spend worthwhile and building trust in your leadership and communication skills. These are basic steps used when conducting a needs assessment:

1. **Review existing data sources:** Find out what is already known and what resources are available regarding your topic.

2. **Formulate needs assessment questions:** What is it you want to know? Also, determine who needs to be included.

3. **Collect data:** Determine what methods you want to use to collect data and decide who will be responsible for data collection.

4. **Analyze your data:** Plan how you will both analyze and display your findings.

5. **Share findings:** Consider a variety of ways to share results publicly.

6. **Use your findings:** Create and enact an action plan based on your findings.

There are several ways to gather data for a needs assessment that we find work well in educational settings. One reason for including multiple types of data in a needs assessment is that different stakeholders may value summative assessment data (e.g., from standardized state or national tests) over formative assessments collected by teachers. Also, because teachers are so immersed in looking at assessment data these days, we have to remember that data can include more than numbers and statistics. In addition to other kinds of assessment data, next we describe four methods for gathering data for a needs assessment: in-person interviews, paper-based or online surveys, focus groups, and telephone or e-mail interviews.

In-person interviews. You can conduct a needs assessment either formally or informally by interviewing people. The goal, however, is to be sure that you interview several people who represent each constituent group relevant to the topic or project. For example, if you are getting ready to design a workshop for all the teachers in your building, you will want to talk not only to classroom teachers from several grade levels and disciplines, but also talk to other staff who will be required to attend or who may be affected. Because this is a needs assessment, you should ask a series of open-ended questions that will help you learn what each group needs and wants to get from your workshop. You can also ask them what ways they learn best and what they think are features of the best workshops they attended previously. Your questions should be open-ended to show that you are honestly seeking their input to learn what will make a good learning experience for them. Using the teaching of writing as an example, you might ask: In what ways do you use writing in your teaching? What do you think students need to learn to become better writers? What do you want to know to become a better teacher of writing? What are some ways you think would help you learn to be a teacher of writing? What do you like and dislike most about participating in professional learning workshops?

It is always a good idea to seek permission before recording what anyone tells you during an interview. If you decide not to use a recording device, you still need some way to capture what you learned, whether you take notes during the interview or right after it. Even if you do your needs assessment by having informal conversations with various stakeholders, you still need to write down your impressions and any specifics you learn before you forget them. Finally, thanking people for their time and input is a respectful way to conclude any interview.

Surveys. You can use a combination of open- and closed-ended questions in a survey to keep respondents focused and to help you obtain the data you need to answer your needs assessment questions, as the examples show in Table 7.1. There are many choices for how you can distribute surveys including paper, an e-mail attachment, or through a link to an online survey tool. It is easy to distribute a survey on paper or send it as an e-mail attachment, but it is also cheap, quick, and easy enough to put your survey online using Google Forms. Or you can use the free version of Survey Monkey at surveymonkey.com, although the free version limits you to 10 questions and a maximum of 100 respondents per survey.

Surveys you create should be brief and to the point so that you get a good response rate, but a 100% response rate is extremely rare. Be prepared to only get about a 40%–50% response rate to most surveys, or even less if you ask too many questions. In all cases, pilot testing your survey questions with a few colleagues will help ensure that you are asking questions in a way that will yield meaningful answers. Ask a colleague or two to check that you are only asking one question at a time, and ask someone to check your spelling and use of jargon that not everyone may understand. It is also important to keep the rating scale on your survey consistent and logical. If you need quantitative data, you can easily translate responses like Strongly Agree, Excellent, or Extremely Helpful as 4 points and Strongly Disagree, Poor, or Very Unhelpful as 1 point. We say this because we do not recommend a 5-point scale with a neutral choice in the middle that won't yield as much information.

TABLE 7.1 Examples of Survey Questions and Answer Choices

QUESTION	FORMATS FOR ANSWER CHOICE
How familiar are you with Writer's Workshop?	Circle one: Not at all A little Somewhat Very familiar 1 2 3 4
What ways would you prefer to use to learn about Writer's Workshop?	Check all that apply: ❑ Face-to-face workshop ❑ Online, self-paced course ❑ Book study/discussion ❑ Other:
Do you currently teach writing at least weekly?	Check one: ❑ Yes ❑ No
Please describe what you would most like to learn about writing instruction.	Describe:

Modified from www.ovcttac.gov/taResources/OVCTAGuides/ConductingNeedsAssessment/pfv.html

Focus groups. Once you gather about five people, together you can have a focus group. However, more than 10 people in a focus group may be too many if you want to keep the time brief and have everyone respond to your questions. Think of this kind of needs assessment as a brief but very focused and purposeful conversation. Begin by thanking those willing to participate. Then explain the purpose of the focus group and how it will proceed. This means explaining how everyone will contribute (orally), how much time you have allotted (keep it brief—maybe 15 minutes), and describing your reasons for recording the session (so you can listen again later, and so you don't miss anything). You could ask a colleague to keep notes or record the key points made in a focus group on chart paper for all to see. Or you can use Google Docs to record key points, which easily can be shared later. Be sure to acknowledge there may be different opinions, which is why you want to hear everyone's thoughts and ideas on the topic. This can be accomplished by explaining the ground rules and your expectations: one speaker at a time, no right or wrong responses to the questions, no side conversations, speaking up to be captured on the recording device.

After introductions (in cases when everyone does not know each other), the first question in a focus group should be, "What are your thoughts about X?" Some other general, open-ended questions could include: Would you say you are satisfied with X? If so, what are you satisfied about? What is going well? What are you not satisfied with? What is not going so well? How might you improve things about X? More specific questions can be asked but they should be open-ended as well (eliminate any yes-no questions), focused on gathering information and ideas, and limited to no more than five or six questions in total. For example, given the teaching of writing example mentioned above, you might ask everyone in a focus group: What are your thoughts about teaching writing? What are some ways you have taught writing that you felt were successful? What didn't work? What are some things you would like to know more about regarding the teaching of writing? What are some ways you learn best?

Having a coleader so that either you or your partner can take notes or record focus group sessions allows you to focus on asking the questions, making sure everyone contributes, and listening carefully in case you also want to ask clarifying questions. In any case, be sure to test your recording device before the focus group begins, and maybe check it briefly during the session as well—just for peace of mind. You also have to remember to start the recording device, so make a note of this at the top of the list of questions you have prepared in advance. Another thing to remember is that providing a snack may encourage participation!

Telephone surveys. Using the telephone to conduct a needs assessment is also an option, especially if you are reaching outside the school to include parents/guardians or other community members. Also, telephone surveys can be done from home. If this is your choice, asking open-ended questions will yield details and examples, while asking questions with a limited choice of answers will allow you to collate and compare data across respondents. In all cases, keeping phone interviews brief is a good practice. Preparing both your questions and an opening script ahead of time is also important.

Using a combination of these methods to conduct a needs assessment may work for you, or you may just choose one way to collect data that makes sense because it is cost efficient and worth the time. For example, you may decide to create an online survey and then share the data with a focus group to further explore the implications of the survey and make recommendations for action. Social media tools like Twitter, Facebook, Instagram, Tumblr, or whatever tool your teachers are currently using, can also be used to help you conduct a quick needs assessment. Table 7.2 provides more information about the pros and cons about several methods that can be used for collecting data for a needs assessment. When selecting a data collection approach for your needs assessment, remember that the ultimate goal is to collect the best information you can to help you provide appropriate data, tackle a problem, assess what is going on, or prepare to initiate a change.

We help teacher leaders develop survey and interview questions as tools for gathering data when they do teacher action research projects. We also ask them to practice these same skills when they are planning for professional development, leading an initiative in their professional learning community (PLC), or considering how to begin a teacher leadership project. We also ask them to use their needs assessment skills to assess how things are going with something already in place before any changes are proposed because purposeful exploration is the basis of the needs assessment.

TABLE 7.2 Pros and Cons of Needs Assessment Methods

METHOD	ADVANTAGES	POTENTIAL CHALLENGES	TIME REQUIRED TO CONDUCT	TIME REQUIRED TO ANALYZE	RESOURCE INTENSITY
In-Person Interviews	You can obtain more detailed information about complex issues, ask follow-up questions immediately, and observe nonverbal communication that can help shape the direction of the interview.	It may cost more time to conduct interviews, and you may have to limit the number of people that you interview.	High	High	Medium to High
Telephone Interviews	You can obtain detailed information from respondents who are geographically dispersed, and you may save costs compared with in-person interviews.	It may be difficult to get someone to talk to you for an extended period. Scheduling phone interview may be difficult.	Medium to High	Medium	Medium
Focus Groups	You are able to convene a group to discuss your topic, and the discussion can yield insightful information generated by the discussion.	Some participants may not feel comfortable sharing their true feelings or knowledge in a group setting.	Medium	High	Medium to High
Surveys	You can solicit specific information from a larger number of people. If you e-mail surveys, you allow people to complete them at a time most convenient for them. You also can administer them online to increase the response rate.	If administered via e-mail, it may be difficult to motivate people to complete and e-mail in the survey, which may result in a lower response rate. Everyone you want to reach may not have access to technology.	Low to Medium	Low	Medium

SOURCE: The authors gratefully acknowledge the Office of Victims of Crimes, the Office of Justice Programs, U.S. Department of Justice, for allowing us to reproduce, in part or in whole, the above information.

ACTIVITY: Given any of these scenarios (planning for professional development, leading a PLC initiative, developing a teacher research project, considering a particular leadership project, evaluating something already in place, proposing a change, or any other scenario you can think of) and considering your workplace: (a) Identify an area in which a needs assessment might be useful and needed. (b) Given your circumstances, determine which type(s) of needs assessment data would be valuable

(Continued)

to collect. In other words, consider what questions you want answers to and what data would be helpful in answering them? (c) List some strategies for completing a needs assessment and share them with your school leader or with another educator. (d) Finally, consider how you might share the data you uncover with others in your workplace. Would you develop a chart, a handout, hold a meeting, or make a presentation? What are other ways to share what you learn from a needs assessment?

When designing a needs assessment it is worth revisiting what you learned about change theory in Chapter 5. We recommend this because responses to some of your needs assessment questions might be analyzed using the levels in the Concerns-Based Adoption Model (CBAM) as a framework for determining both what you as a leader and others are concerned about. You can also use CBAM to create questions to determine the level of comfort with a current innovation, or determine what concerns a group you are working with might have with a new innovation. The pay-off is that when you do a needs assessment using CBAM as a guide, you will be able to determine if you should start at the beginning or if you can skip a few levels because your constituents already have answers to some of their early concerns and questions. This framework can also be used to guide you when planning for various professional learning experiences.

The process of developing interview or survey questions in the following activity is not only suitable when conducting a needs assessment, but it is also suitable for teacher leaders planning a teacher action research project or a teacher leadership project.

ACTIVITY: **(a)** Design 10 interview questions and 10 survey questions to be used for a needs assessment about an authentic topic that is of interest to you. **(b)** Share the first draft of your questions with a peer or two to get feedback before revising them. **(c)** Pilot test both your interview and survey questions with a few people or a small focus group, or send out your revised survey questions to a few people as a pilot. As part of piloting interview and survey questions, be sure to add a final question that asks specifically for any feedback on the quality or structure of the interview or survey itself. **(d)** Use the information from pilot testing your data collection instruments to revise and finalize your interview and survey questions.

HOW DO YOU PLAN, DELIVER, AND EVALUATE PROFESSIONAL LEARNING ACTIVITIES?

Once you see a need for professional learning, or whenever you are asked to lead others in a professional learning activity (e.g., workshop, presentation, book club, online discussion, etc.), a needs assessment should be the first thing that comes to mind as part of planning, delivering, and evaluating any form of professional learning. "The effectiveness of any professional learning activity, regardless of its content, structure, or format, depends mainly on how well it is planned" (Guskey, 2014, p. 12). Referring to the six steps listed earlier in this chapter for undertaking a needs assessment, the first thing is to determine what is already known about the topic, including both what you know and what others know. This includes considering what resources are available regarding the topic. This will lead to further data gathering, whether this includes interviewing or surveying people from relevant groups, or conducting focus groups or telephone surveys/interviews. Launching into planning for what content to cover and how to do so is premature without finding out what people already know and what they want to know. As insiders, teacher leaders already have a lot of insight about the needs and wants of other teachers in their buildings, but you should not assume that you know everything without consulting others. In addition, consulting others helps you build relationships and find allies, making your efforts more focused and well received because you did a needs assessment. The time and effort will pay off!

Once you have determined what you know, what others know and need, what resources are available, and have collected and analyzed some needs assessment data, then planning to lead professional learning opportunities can begin in earnest. However, it should be noted that these steps need not be taken in a linear, sequential manner because in reality many of these steps can be accomplished simultaneously. However, leaving out any of the steps may mean you will miss or misunderstand something, or that you will not do the best job possible. Also referring back to what you learned in Chapter 4 about working with adults, including adults from different generations, will help you remember to incorporate the tips we suggested for planning and delivering professional learning experiences and leading other adult colleagues. This means exercising your metacognitive thinking about how adults learn, meeting their needs by acknowledging and making use of their prior knowledge and experiences, making learning experiences active and interactive, meeting their need for affiliation and connection, and considering that everyone has different learning styles. Knowing what kind of role(s) you want to take on as a leader and following the practical tips about working with adult learners provided in Tables 4.3 and 4.4 are also recommended, as are the skills discussed in Chapter 6 about facilitating groups, managing time, and even resolving conflict.

Making use of technology as part of your planning for professional learning is always a good idea and could easily be included in your needs assessment. In fact, because of its versatility, various kinds of technology can be used in planning, delivering, and evaluating professional learning opportunities. For example, you could use Google tools (see Chapter 6) such as e-mail or Google+, Google Forms, Google Docs, Google Slides, and Google Sites to do your needs assessment, to collaboratively design and share a presentation or other materials, to archive materials for continued access, and to evaluate the success of the professional learning experience you led. Social media tools like Twitter, and whatever else your teachers are currently using, can also be used to help you do a needs assessment, plan, and evaluate professional learning opportunities. We also suggest additional tools for planning, delivering, and evaluating professional learning in Table 7.3, although you can probably think of even more technology tools to add to our suggestions. Furthermore, it is worth remembering that some technology tools can serve multiple purposes and that some are free, so choose wisely.

There are also many cloud storage apps (e.g., Dropbox, OneDrive), social bookmarking sites (e.g., Del.icio.us, Symbaloo) that are useful for collecting websites as you plan and for sharing them with others. There are also back-channel tools (e.g., Backchannelchat, TodaysMeet, or Socrative) that encourage teachers to engage and interact during a session in a variety of ways—asking questions, making comments and suggestions, answering your questions. There are also many content websites and videos that can be used for professional learning, so ask about favorite technology websites as part of your needs assessment and then add these to your repertoire.

TABLE 7.3 Technology for Planning, Delivering, and Evaluating Professional Learning

PLANNING TOOLS	DELIVERY TOOLS	EVALUATION TOOLS
• Edmodo or Moodle as a learning management tool	• Animoto or Replay	• Animoto or Replay
• Evernote or Padlet	• Edmodo or Moodle as a learning management tool	• Edmodo
• Glogster	• Glogster	• Bighugelabs.com
• Inspiration or Bubbl.us or Popplet	• Interactive White Board like Promethean or Smart	• Glogster
• LiveBinders	• Inspiration or Bubbl.us or Popplet	• Inspiration or Bubbl.us or Popplet
• Pinterest	• LiveBinders	• Padlet or Evernote
• Survey Monkey	• Pinterest	• Poll Everywhere
• Twitter	• PowerPoint, Prezi, SlideRocket, or Keynote	• Socrative
• Personal Learning Networks (PLNs)	• Voicethread	• Survey Monkey
		• TodaysMeet
		• Twitter

As for actually planning the professional learning opportunities you will lead, Guskey (2014) recommends using backward planning (see Wiggins & McTighe, 2005) because "you must clarify the goals you want to achieve in terms of better educator practice and improved student learning before you can judge the value, worth, and appropriateness of any professional learning activity" (p. 13). Based on our own experience, we concur, so this means starting with the end in mind—that is, starting with your goals—which Guskey advocates should always be focused on desired student learning outcomes. Goal setting needs to happen before you choose any new practices you want to instill and support to improve the knowledge and skills teachers need to improve student learning. Next is deciding what kinds of formative assessments you will use to determine if your participants learned what you intended. Last on the list when planning backward are the actual learning activities you might use and the best way(s) to structure teacher learning. This is backward because most teachers naturally think about activities first before considering what outcomes they want from the activities. However, this is not ideal because while the learning activities may be fun, engaging, and interactive, they may not achieve the ultimate goals of teacher learning that will lead to improved student learning. As Guskey (2014) so clearly stated, "Before thinking about the format and content of any professional learning experience, we must first consider the specific student learning outcomes we want to attain and what evidence will best reflect those outcomes" (p. 14). Guskey continued,

> Some educators contend that improving student learning outcomes represents too lofty a goal for many professional learning activities. Those in education service agencies and state or district offices, for example, often indicate they are too far removed from classroom interactions to expect their efforts to consistently reach that level. Because of this distance, they should only be accountable for providing evidence that the professional learning activities they plan and coordinate improve educators' knowledge and skills. But if these professional learning activities increase educators' knowledge and skills but result in no change in school or classroom practice and no improvements in student learning, would we consider these activities successful? In almost every instance, the answer is a resounding "No!" So even at these levels, planning needs to begin with discussions of intended effects on student learning. (p. 14)

Once the goals for professional learning are established, then it is important to remember what else we know about effective professional learning. We know it should be (1) job-embedded (occur locally at the school level during the regular workday and be relevant to teachers' responsibilities); (2) research-based and standards-driven; (3) focused on grade-level and/or discipline-specific content and skills; (4) include effective demonstrations and multiple opportunities for active engagement and practice with feedback; and (5) be followed up with ongoing coaching and feedback. In addition, professional learning must include adequate (6) time for collaborative analysis and reflection on student work, student assessment data, and current teaching practices; (7) time for sharing successful teaching strategies along with learning content and new teaching strategies; and (8) time for collaboration, co-planning, and problem solving.

Given this list of what makes for effective professional learning, old-fashioned, one-shot, "sit and get" time after school "training" sessions are not sufficient for teachers to improve their practice, much less for there to be any impact on student learning. Instead, teacher leaders must work to plan and deliver, or better yet to collaboratively plan and co-facilitate professional learning opportunities that include the above eight characteristics. Then, and only then, should they be concerned about specific activities that will meet these criteria and the ultimate goals of teacher learning and student achievement.

ACTIVITY: Take the time to plan how professional learning about teacher leadership could look in your workplace. Think about the various self-assessment surveys you have completed to this point, and your own ideas for what colleagues you work with should know about teacher leadership. Then work with at least one partner or a small group to design a needs assessment about a teacher leadership initiative. Once you have the results of the needs assessment, begin planning some professional learning opportunities for teachers using backward design so that every teacher can begin to think about becoming a leader.

WHAT SKILLS DO YOU NEED FOR SUCCESSFUL GRANT WRITING?

As with leading professional learning, grant writing should never be a solitary effort. However, it often takes someone to lead the effort. The skills needed to ensure success in writing a grant are actually very basic: careful reading of the grant's guidelines, following directions, and meeting deadlines. Everyone can do these basic things, but it helps to have good ideas and a passion for what you are seeking to fund through a grant. We encourage you to show leadership in this area—first in your classroom and then in your school—ideally with other people. However, finding funding for grants can be a challenge, which we address below.

We find that it is kind of a chicken-or-egg issue about whether you should first have a project and a plan regarding what you need a grant to fund, or whether you should go searching for funding opportunities and then develop your project and plan. Teacher leaders we have worked with have done this both ways with good success. However, receiving a grant means you actually have to accomplish what you said you would do when applying for a grant. Therefore, it is important that you are passionate about your idea and that it is a worthwhile use of your time and the funder's money. Remember that a needs assessment regarding a possible grant would be worth your time, and we share several additional grant-writing tips in Table 7.4, which you should add to the basics of careful reading, following directions, and meeting deadlines.

As mentioned above, one thing that often slows teachers down is learning where to find grants and where to find additional help writing grants. Table 7.5 includes several websites to use as a starting point for finding grants and additional websites that provide additional grant writing tips.

TABLE 7.4   Grant-Writing Tips

As soon as you have a *project* idea and *permission* to implement it, use the following to formulate your *plans*:

- **Background:** Document the need for your project with demographics, test results, and anecdotal evidence. Here is where a needs assessment fits in.

- **Mission statement:** Identify the project's potential outcome, which means doing some backward planning.

- **Goals and objectives:** Make sure they are specific and measurable as you plan ways to gather data to assess the success of the grant.

- **Timeline:** Be realistic.

- **Planned assessment tool(s):** Design these at the start and consider gathering several forms of assessment: summative and formative, quantitative and qualitative.

- **Required materials, supplies, and personnel:** Include these in the total cost.

After you get a grant:

- **Write a thank you note** to the grant funder and to your contact person.

- Adhere to the **specifications and timeline** presented in the grant application.

- Be ready to **write a final report** about the outcomes of the grant.

TABLE 7.5   Resources for Finding Grant Sources Online

Links to MANY Grant Opportunities:

- www.neafoundation.org/pages/resources-other-grant-opportunities
  - www.getedfunding.com
  - www.grantsforteachers.net

Donors Choose: www.donorschoose.org/teachers

Pledge Cents: www.pledgecents.com/

Target Grant FAQs: corporate.target.com/corporate-responsibility/grants/grants-faq

- **Target Funds Field Trips:** Target funds field trips up to $700 that connect students' classroom curricula to out-of-school experiences. Field trips must take place between February and December. Target Field Trip Grants applications are accepted Aug. 1–Sept. 30.

NEA Foundation Grants to Educators: http://www.neafoundation.org/pages/grants-to-educators/

- Deadlines for applications are due February 1, June 1, and October 15.

Links to even more grant opportunities:

- www.libraryspot.com/features/grantsfeature.htm

Excellent online resources about successful grant writing:

- www2.guidestar.org/rxa/news/articles/2003/what-grantmakers-want-applicants-to-know.aspx
- www.educationworld.com/a_admin/grants/grant_help.shtml

We always include grant writing in our work with teacher leaders to encourage them to find and write a grant—either for their classroom, their grade or department, or their school. We suggest starting by applying for local grants or something like DonorsChoose.org rather than going for a National Science Foundation grant, for example. Teachers can also look into their national disciplinary organizations, such as the NCTM Grant Opportunities for Math (http://www.nctm.org/Grants/). Partnering with a local college or university, or with local businesses, is also worth considering. Many of the teacher leaders we work with have already been successful with writing grants and can share their experiences and advice with others. Winning a grant seems to motivate teachers to pursue grants rather than spend their own money, and teacher leaders can pull people together to do this. Success seems to breed success, and we have seen that grant-writing skills improve with practice. Therefore, our advice is to go for it!

As a result of including grant writing as a skill teacher leaders need to develop, we have had several teacher leaders provide workshops and ongoing support to help teachers in their schools write grants. In one great example of teacher leadership, Jennifer helped 12 teachers at her elementary school receive grants to fund over 20 projects worth more than $8,000 in just one year. One teacher in her school successfully submitted and won five grants. Here are some of the comments Jennifer received from her colleague, Caitlin:

> *Hey! You have done a great job promoting and getting everyone more aware of Donor's Choose. Although Donor's Choose was mentioned to me a couple years ago, I didn't have the motivation to really go through with it. My project just sat there until it had been archived. Seeing the success you had with the projects you have posted, made me more motivated to put one in. You took your time to help me with my annoying and tedious questions—from how to navigate through the site, how to locate the items I am searching for, and even wording to be used for my project. You also provided me with multiple tips in order to make my project successful! It worked and I have gotten my project funded!! Thank you for your time with it all and the motivation. Thank you for all that you do for our babies!*

WHAT SKILLS ARE NEEDED FOR EFFECTIVE ADVOCACY AND OUTREACH?

Once teacher leaders learn more about how to reach out and get grants for their classroom or school, and once they learn how educational policies are enacted from those who are engaged in this work (see Chapter 5), we ask them to develop additional skills needed to become advocates. We ask them to write an advocacy piece. We provide them with tips for writing their advocacy pieces, talk about using appropriate language and tone, and provide them with e-mail and/or mailing addresses for their local school board members, superintendent, local newspaper, state legislative representatives, governor, and so on. However, we always let them choose what they would like to advocate for, who they think the audience for their advocacy efforts should be, and what form or format they would like their advocacy piece to take, as we describe in this activity:

ACTIVITY: Write a persuasive essay, op-ed piece, or letter of advocacy about a particular issue related to teachers, teaching, or teacher leadership about which you have a strong opinion. Select any one of these people or groups as your audience: principal, parents, local school board, newspaper, school of education dean at your local university or alma mater, state board of education or state superintendent of schools, member of the state legislature, the governor, and so on. Be sure to back up your opinion with data and/or facts and conclude with a concrete suggestion or two related to improving the issue, the teaching profession, and/or advancing teacher leadership. Follow the bulleted points below, which we learned from a local policy wonk, to structure your advocacy piece.

- Describe your concern, issue, or request in simple, clear language.
- If writing about specific legislation, say: "I am a constituent who cares about SB 5."
- State how you are personally affected.
- Offer your opinion in the first 1 to 2 sentences.
- Give 2 to 3 facts to back your opinion and/or provide links to 1 to 2 relevant articles.
- Avoid using educational jargon or acronyms.
- Demonstrate respect and courtesy throughout.
- If writing to state or federal legislators, include your address, so they know you are a constituent.
- If you have any personal association with policymakers, remind them of this connection.

In one of our states, the legislature recently passed a law restricting teachers (in fact, all state employees) from using any school (state) resources, or any of the time during which they are employed to engage in advocacy. Therefore, we now ask teachers to write their advocacy pieces at home. Nevertheless, we think it is important for teacher leaders to learn how to speak up and write about policy issues that affect them. At the very least we ask them to share their advocacy piece with peers to get their feedback, and we encourage (but do not require) them to actually send their advocacy pieces. (See the companion website for examples of advocacy.)

Outreach and advocacy can also be done face-to-face and through the use of technology. Therefore, learning the skill of creating cogent bullet points about an educational issue or need is valuable because we know policymakers and grant funders have limited time and are faced with many requests and varying perspectives. Writing executive summaries and using bullet points effectively are more advanced communication skills teacher leaders should learn. The issue is one of considering your audience, so we ask teacher leaders to practice writing one-page, executive summaries about their grant-writing efforts, their advocacy interests, or about their perspective on an educational policy in the news.

Writing an executive summary. Executive summaries are typically one-page documents that include the purpose of the communication, a statement of the problem, and a summary of results, conclusions, and recommendations. Often the content of an executive summary is selected from a larger document, but an executive summary is somewhat different from an abstract. An abstract offers a very brief summary of research or a report including an overview of main points, methods, results, and implications. Often abstracts are limited to 100–150 words, and they are used mainly in academia, while executive summaries are more often used in government, science, education, and business. One reason for writing an executive summary is to provide all the important facts and figures on one page. Another reason is to capture the main points of a longer document for someone who may not have time to read the entire report. Executive summaries should be concise (often achieved by using bullet points, headings, and graphics), reader friendly for the target audience, contain no jargon, and should make sense even if you have not read the original report. It takes some practice with the skill of summarizing to write an executive summary, so we provide some tips in Table 7.6. However, it helps to start by answering these questions as you write an executive summary:

- Who is the audience for your executive summary?
- What are the main ideas you want and need to present?
- What is the purpose, key findings, or thesis to be conveyed in a one-page summary?
- What recommendations or suggestions are crucial to include?
- What are the strengths and weaknesses of the recommendations?
- What graphics can you use to convey information concisely?
- What information can be bulleted to keep the summary quick and easy to read?

TABLE 7.6 Tips for Writing an Executive Summary

When your executive summary is a summary of a larger document

- Start with the original document
- Read and become familiar with the original document
- Condense the informative to include the main ideas
- Write a brief summary using short paragraphs, headings, bullet points, and graphics, if available, that convey information concisely

If your executive summary is to support a grant idea, or designed to help support your advocacy for an educational issue or policy

- Define the problem you are addressing
- Support your claims with facts and statistics
- Explain your unique solution(s)
- Include a brief example or anecdote to enhance your unique solution(s)
- Make sure your summary contains no jargon and is error free
- Proofread for clarity, coherence, forcefulness, and conciseness

Creating an elevator speech. We also ask teacher leaders to write, memorize, and share a 30-second "elevator speech" about their grant requests, about an educational policy that affects teachers and students, or to share good news about their school to share with others—visitors to their school, parents, families, school board members, legislators, and so on. Fine tuning your executive summary can help with preparing an elevator speech, as long as you remember to do the following: eliminate any jargon, select just a few facts and details to emphasize, make sentences short but powerful, connect your points, and get rid of any unnecessary words. Remember that your elevator speech has to sound natural and flow smoothly. Therefore, it is important to memorize your key points, practice it, and not rush when delivering an elevator speech. A well-planned elevator speech prepares you for knowing just what to say if you have only a short amount of time to capture someone's attention and deliver your message. You never know when you might have the opportunity to reach out to someone who might help your school, when you might have a chance to influence someone about both the needs and the positives in education, or have a chance to advocate for teacher leadership. Having that 30-second elevator speech ready shows skill as a teacher leader. Table 7.7 includes tips for preparing a 30-second elevator speech with an example.

TABLE 7.7 Tips With Examples for an Elevator Speech

- Smile and introduce yourself briefly. State what you do enthusiastically.

  EXAMPLE: *Hi, I am Samantha Smith, and I am a passionate, fifth-year math teacher at Washington Middle School.*

- Ask a question or make a statement that grabs attention. Ideally, you want to hook your listener's interest and prompt him or her to ask questions.

  EXAMPLE: *Do you know that I have not received a raise in the last five years? Do you think people in any other profession would remain in their job with no raises?*

  or

  EXAMPLE: *I represent the 30% to 50% of teachers who leave the classroom by their fifth year, taking more than $50,000 dollars of professional development you have invested in me.*

- Share a problem you have solved or a contribution you have made.

  EXAMPLE: *All my students made growth in my math classes last year thanks in part to my being able to attend the state math conference every year.*

(Continued)

TABLE 7.7 (Continued)

- Offer a powerful example.

  EXAMPLE: *In the past three years every one of my ESL students made more than a year's growth in math because I learned how to reach them by hearing about what other teachers do.*

- Explain why you are interested in your listener.

  EXAMPLE: *I want your assurance that you will advocate for new options to support teacher leaders in our schools because I want to share what I am doing to make my math students so successful.*

- Suggest a solution to the problem or concern you expressed.

  EXAMPLE: *I propose that teacher leaders be supported in this state with additional financial compensation for their efforts so that they do not leave the classroom.*

  or

  EXAMPLE: *Therefore, I am proposing that all teachers be funded annually to attend a state or national professional conference to support their professional learning.*

- Give a concrete example or tell a short story to further your point.

  EXAMPLE: *I know that in several other states teacher leaders spend half their time teaching and half their time on teacher leadership activities such as mentoring other teachers, working on curriculum development, or giving workshops for other teachers. Known as teacherpreneurs, they not only keep their salary and benefits, they sometimes get a 10% to 12% pay raise for their leadership efforts.*

- Explain the advantages of working with you.

  EXAMPLE: *If you want teachers to vote for you in the next election, you are going to have to work toward finding ways to support teachers who want to become leaders by helping other teachers improve their practice.*

- Determine what response you want after your elevator speech and ask for it.

  EXAMPLE: *Please tell me what plans you have for supporting teacher leadership during this legislative session?*

You can use these tools and your new skills to advocate for your school because what you have to say is a form of advertising. Once you have either an executive summary or your elevator speech polished, you have the content needed to reach out through your school's website, a blog post, or on Twitter to advocate for your position, cause, or project. You can also use these skills to convince a potential funder to give you money, and maybe even persuade a policymaker or legislator to see your point of view. With some practice—perhaps with colleagues in your school—you will have the skills needed for effective advocacy and outreach as a teacher leader.

HOW DO YOU USE DATA AND REFLECTIVE PRACTICE AS A TEACHER LEADER?

We believe that all teachers are naturally reflective about their students and their practice. We certainly remember reflecting while in the shower, while driving to and from school, when planning lessons, and when talking with colleagues. We also reflect in the moment when a lesson isn't proceeding as planned, or we see that not every student understands. Schön (1983, 1987) called this reflecting "in action" and reflecting "on action"; that is, we reflect "in action" while we are in the act of teaching and interacting with our students, and we reflect "on action" after the lesson or the day is over—either on our own or with a colleague.

Today, teachers are encouraged to reflect about not just teaching their lessons, but on the data they and others are constantly collecting about their students. These data might come from formal and informal assessments that are either teacher-created or produced by publishers, or by district or state personnel. Data about students can come from many sources: fluency checks, reading inventories, observations, checklists, spelling tests, weekly quizzes, work samples, parents, quarterly assessments, benchmarks, progress monitoring, scores on rubrics, common assessments, and standardized tests of all kinds. In fact, teachers and teacher leaders are inundated with data that they must understand, reflect on, and then act on to help all their students continue to learn. How do you use data and reflective practice as a teacher leader?

One role for teacher leaders is to learn how to make use of the data they and their colleagues have. It is one thing to develop your skill in understanding data, which is beyond the scope of this book, but it is another thing to interpret and know what to do with data. This is where your leadership skills, your experience, and your growing ability to think metacognitively about your teaching can come into play. In addition, teacher leaders must display positive dispositions, critical thinking, and problem solving when using data to help understand what is going on with their students. They must also understand that everyone's students are their responsibility, not just the students in their classes. To help develop and exercise positive dispositions about using data and being reflective practitioners, we recommend the following model for thinking about data.

Table 7.8 describes each step in the Data Wise process, which we see as an excellent process that teacher leaders can use to show leadership. You can do this yourself and help others learn how to make use of data in a collaborative manner with the goal of improving teaching and increasing learning for all. Teacher leaders can reflect on and lead others through each step in the Data Wise process after learning more about this process by reading *Data Wise, Revised and Expanded Edition: A Step-by-Step Guide to Using Assessment Results to Improve Teaching and Learning* by Kathryn Boudett, Elizabeth City, and Richard Murnane (2013). Even better, they can read and discuss this book with others in a book club or book study group they help organize. In addition, anyone can participate in a massive open online course (MOOC) that is available free through www.edX.org to learn more about this process. Because teacher leaders are disposed to be lifelong learners, participating in an open, online learning community like this MOOC is a great way to demonstrate their disposition to be a learner as well as a teacher. In fact, sharing this

TABLE 7.8 Purpose of Each Step of the Data Wise Improvement Process

STEP	PURPOSE OF THIS STEP	HOW THIS STEP PLAYED OUT AT HIGHLAND ACADEMY
1. Organize for collaborative work.	Establish structures and teams.	Schoolwide meeting agenda template and norms
2. Build assessment literacy.	Increase comfort with data.	Professional development on interpreting assessment reports related to literacy, the schoolwide focus area
3. Create data overview.	Identify a priority question.	"How do students approach finding the main idea in literature?"
4. Dig into student data.	Identify a learner-centered problem.	"When answering questions about literature, students tend to zoom in on characters and their feelings about them without stepping back to consider the main idea of the story."
5. Examine instruction.	Identify a problem of practice.	"As teachers, we tend to 'give away' the main idea of a story at the beginning of a lesson and devote most class time to encouraging students to identify personal connections to the characters."
6. Develop action plan.	Create an action plan.	Instructional Strategy: Close analytic reading
7. Plan to assess progress.	Create a plan to assess progress.	Short-term: In-class presentations Medium-term: Teacher-designed written assessments Long-term: State English Language Arts assessment
8. Act and assess.	Document improvements in teaching and learning and adjust as needed.	After implementing the instructional strategy, teachers noticed that students improved in their ability to identify the main idea orally but struggled to capture it in writing. Teachers continued to adjust their instruction, and by the end of the year most students were proficient in the "main idea" sub-skill on the state test.

Used with permission from ASCD.

information with other teachers, or getting a group of teachers together to participate in the MOOC, would make a great leadership project.

You may already be using this process as a protocol for looking at data, but if not we highly recommend it. If you are already following this process when analyzing student data, consider conducting a needs assessment to see if your team is using each of these steps effectively. This will help you determine if the time you spend evaluating student data is being used wisely. If not, show leadership by determining where and how your process could be improved.

SUMMARY

This chapter focused on additional skills teacher leaders need to enhance their efforts to lead. These include skills needed to conduct needs assessments, plan and deliver professional learning opportunities, write winning grants, and successfully engage in advocacy and outreach activities. Some of these skills are very basic and some more advanced, but all are ultimately about communication and collaboration, which are key skills needed by all teacher leaders. We also addressed the importance of teacher leaders being reflective and using data, and presented a framework known as the Data Wise Improvement Process to guide teacher leaders in helping themselves and others make use of data to improve student learning in their workplace. Additional activities, readings, and scenarios, and questions for reflection and discussion are available in the companion website for this book.

CHAPTER 8

The Future of
Teacher Leadership

Teacher leadership must be a force for changing education—not a result of it.

—Andrew Varga

VIEW FROM A SCHOOL LEADER	VIEW FROM A TEACHER LEADER
Mrs. Brown, I have to say that our conversations have made me think more about the future of teacher leadership at our school. I know you have the right dispositions to make a great teacher leader, but I also know you and other potential teacher leaders need to develop your knowledge and skills if you are going to thrive as teacher leaders. In fact, I am thinking this is something we should put on our agenda to discuss more—not just the school improvement team's agenda, but the agenda for our staff meetings. What do you think?	Mr. Peterson, I agree completely. I think we should all be talking more and learning more about teacher leadership. There are so many teachers in our school who could be great leaders. Like me, however, I bet they have lots of questions and feel like they need to know more. They need your support, and they definitely need some professional development about the dispositions, knowledge, and skills needed for teacher leadership. What are some ways we could all learn more about teacher leadership?

This chapter focuses on the future of teacher leadership, including examples of what teacher leaders can accomplish and ideas for increasing teacher leadership in schools. Suggestions for how school and district leaders can support teacher leaders are included in this chapter as well. In addition, two different agendas for professional development around teacher leadership are suggested. These range from half-day workshops to a year-long learning experience, but there are many other ways to use the content of this book to guide professional learning experiences for both active and prospective teacher leaders. Specific questions answered in this chapter include:

1. What is the future of teacher leadership?

2. What can schools accomplish with strong teacher leadership?

3. What can school and district leaders do to support teacher leadership?

4. What are some professional development models for preparing more teacher leaders?

According to the MetLife Survey of American Teachers (2013), job satisfaction has dropped to the lowest level in over 25 years. In fact, teachers' job satisfaction has dropped 23 points since 2008, including a 5% drop since the previous year's survey, to the point that only 39% of teachers reported being very satisfied with their job. The job satisfaction of principals has also dropped. Further, both teachers and principals with low job satisfaction tend to be working in high-need schools where they report experiencing stress, diminishing budgets, and less time for professional development and collaboration (MetLife, 2013). In addition,

> The survey underscores the fact that teachers today play a key part in the leadership of their schools. Half of teachers now function in formal leadership roles such as department chair, instructional resource, teacher mentor, or leadership team member. These teacher leaders are more likely than others to feel that an effective principal should be able to develop a strong teaching capacity across a school, share leadership with teachers and other staff, and evaluate teachers using multiple measures. Few teachers want to become principals, but half are interested in hybrid, part-time classroom teaching combined with other roles in their school or district. (MetLife, 2013, p. 4)

In sum, 51% of teachers surveyed expressed being somewhat interested in teaching part-time and combining their classroom responsibilities with other roles or responsibilities in their school or district, and 23% expressed being extremely or very interested in combining classroom teaching with other leadership roles (MetLife, 2013). Even Secretary of Education Arne Duncan recently wrote that he was "encouraged" by hybrid positions for teacher leaders.

Unfortunately, 65% of teachers reported that time for collaboration decreased or remained the same in the past year, and 63% said opportunities for professional development also decreased or remained the same as last year. Given that successful teacher leadership requires collaboration with others and that teacher leaders both need and deserve opportunities to develop their leadership skills, these findings present a dilemma for the future of teacher leadership. Given that more than half of teachers want opportunities to lead and principals need all the help they can get, we need to be discussing the future of teacher leadership, addressing what could be accomplished with strong teacher leadership, detailing what can be done to support teacher leaders, and suggesting possible models for developing teacher leaders. These are among the goals of this chapter.

WHAT IS THE FUTURE OF TEACHER LEADERSHIP?

Because teachers with lower job satisfaction are likely to be mid-career teachers rather than new teachers (MetLife, 2013), we must do something to retain both new and experienced teachers. Building their capacity as teacher leaders is one way to do this. We need to support and retain experienced teachers who are already leading in many ways, or who are looking for opportunities to lead beyond their classrooms or schools, and we must prepare the next generation of teacher leaders.

We know that teachers are the most important school-related factor affecting student achievement (Darling-Hammond, 2000; Rice, 2003; Wenglinsky, 2002), so we must nurture teachers and continue to help them grow. We also know that principals want and need to share the work of leading their schools (Levin & Schrum, 2012; MetLife, 2013) because they understand that they cannot accomplish everything on their own. However, there is a fine balance to be considered when talking about teacher leadership so that the goals of teacher leadership always include supporting student achievement and improving schools. Therefore, from our perspective, the goal of promoting teacher leadership definitely is not about encouraging teachers to leave the classroom to be a leader. Rather, it is about leveraging their strengths and developing their expertise in ways that support them as professionals so they can serve their students *and* contribute to their schools at the same time.

Fortunately, there is a growing cry for teacher leadership coming from several places, including a variety of professional educational organizations, teachers' unions, some states and the federal government, and from teachers themselves (c.f. Angelle, 2007; Berry & Teachersolutions 2030 Team, 2011; Berry, Byrd, & Wieder, 2013; Danielson, 2006; Katzenmeyer & Moller, 2009). Today, these discussions go well beyond talking about career ladders, differentiated pay scales, or pay for performance. They are more about changing the way we think about what teachers can do, want opportunities to do, and their need to make a difference during their career.

> *Teacher leadership is about leveraging teachers' strengths and developing their expertise in ways that support them as professionals so they can serve their students and contribute to their schools at the same time.*

As mentioned in another chapter, Berry et al. (2013) described a type of teacher leader they called a teacherpreneur—someone who remains in the classroom at least part-time but also leads outside the classroom—or as they put it "innovative leaders who lead but don't leave" (p. xv). Teacherpreneurs are classroom experts who not only teach regularly but also make time to generate and share their ideas about education: sometimes by teaching in the mornings and working on curriculum projects, by mentoring other teachers, or by leading professional development in the afternoons; sometimes by serving as both a teacher and a leader in a small school; sometimes by teaching K–12 students in the morning and community college or preservice teachers in the afternoons or evenings; and sometimes by teaching online so they have a more flexible schedule for leadership projects with their unions, professional, or state organizations. This kind of teacher leadership requires creative thinking and support from school and district leaders, but it opens our minds to what teacher leadership might look like in the future.

No matter the form teacher leadership might take for you, the Center for Teaching Quality (CTQ, see teachingquality.org) offers ongoing support to teacher leaders through online collaboration among over 9,400 teacher leaders, up from a few dozen in 2003. CTQ hosts a growing number of blogs written by teacher leaders, and an online collaboratory (which is an online discussion board) for networking among teachers with mutual interests in leadership and other aspects of teaching. CTQ also does advocacy work and provides resources for teacher leaders including reports based on ongoing work on educational policy and research. This type of support for teacher leadership is definitely needed, and it is readily available.

CTQ recently partnered with the National Education Association (NEA) and the National Board for Professional Teaching Standards (NBPTS) to create a Teacher Leadership Initiative (TLI) designed to advance teacher leadership in the next generation of teachers. The long-term goals of the TLI include defining the competencies needed by teacher leaders, finding ways to help teachers develop those competencies, and galvanizing teachers to be leaders by undertaking capstone projects connected to either instructional leadership, policy leadership, or association leadership. One hundred and fifty educators from Arizona, Colorado, Iowa, Massachusetts, Michigan, and Mississippi were chosen for the 2014 pilot year, and six more states or districts participated in the second pilot year, including 300 teachers from Arizona, Colorado, Hawaii, Iowa, Maryland, Massachusetts, Michigan, Minnesota, Mississippi, Montana, Ohio, and Utah.

The NEA is also working to empower teachers to lead, shape educational policy, and prepare the next generation of teacher leaders. To do this NEA has partnered with Teach Plus (teachplus.org) to provide fellowships for early career, solutions-oriented teachers who will advise the NEA leadership about teacher engagement and retention. Teach Plus is also providing training and fellowships through several initiatives for teachers in urban areas who are interested in having a voice in educational policy without leaving the classroom. One of these initiatives, known as T3, or Turnaround Teacher Teams, is focused on preparing teacher leaders who can help their peers in high-needs schools improve their instructional practices with the goal of increasing student achievement. This initiative includes training, coaching, and stipends for the extra work involved, and it keeps T3 teacher leaders in their schools.

The Teach Plus C2 initiative is another opportunity for emerging teacher leaders to learn from each other and selected experts about how to best implement standards-based instructional strategies and practices to promote student learning and achievement. As with the T3 initiative that supports Teaching Policy Fellows, C2 teachers are provided training and support as they develop courses for other teachers to help them better teach their standards-based curriculum, including the Common Core. While these teacher leadership initiatives are limited in scope because they only touch a small percentage of the potential pool of teacher leaders in this country, they do grow teacher leaders and they do provide models for what the future of teacher leadership might include.

In addition, the U.S. Department of Education (DOE) has initiated several projects designed to reimagine the profession that prominently include encouraging teacher leadership. One example is Project RESPECT (www.ed.gov/teaching/national-conversation), which has among its goals creating a national conversation among educators to serve as a catalyst for transforming the profession of education through nationwide discussions among teachers and other stakeholders. RESPECT is an acronym for Recognizing Educational Success, Professional Excellence, and Collaborative Teaching. It states as one of its goals "[a] new vision of the profession would offer accomplished teachers multiple pathways to advance their careers without leaving the classroom" (U.S. Department of Education, 2012, p. 10). Additional goals of Project RESPECT include envisioning new models for classroom instruction, increased use of technology to support learning and teaching, changes to the structure of the traditional school day and school year, and creating new school environments that include shared responsibilities and distributed leadership. In its vision statement, which remains a work in progress, the RESPECT project includes the following points, among others, that are relevant to the future of teacher leadership:

- Creating career and leadership opportunities that enable teachers to develop their roles and responsibilities without leaving the classroom.

- Linking teachers' pay to the quality of their work and the scope of their professional responsibilities rather than just years of service.

- Having salaries that reflect the additional challenges of working in high-need schools in urban and rural areas.

- Ensuring that teachers are well supported by principals who respect their expertise and create positive school cultures with high expectations for everyone.

- Assuring that school culture is built on shared responsibility and ongoing collaboration, rather than a top-down authoritarian style.

- Hiring effective principals who are fully engaged in developing and supporting teachers, who involve teachers in leadership decisions, and who provide teachers with authentic, job-embedded professional learning.

- Nurturing creativity and innovation in our schools and classrooms.

- Supporting inclusive schools and classrooms based on students' needs and teachers' abilities, rather than on traditionally prescribed formulas such as seniority (U.S. Department of Education, 2012, 2013).

Figure 8.1 shows Project RESPECT's current model for developing teacher leaders. This flowchart suggests how teachers might progress through different stages of their career. When they become teacher leaders and master teachers, they can stay in their classrooms and schools rather than become principals or take on other positions in their districts that take them out of the classroom.

One specific suggestion made in a Project RESPECT document included several ways to restructure classroom instruction that could support teacher leadership. The ideas include smaller classes for students with special needs and larger classes taught by the most accomplished teachers supported by beginning teachers who simultaneously learn from these accomplished teachers. Classrooms might also be restructured to take advantage of technology as a teaching and learning tool for supporting students working independently or in small groups rather than everyone doing the same thing at the same time. Such restructuring could both actively engage students in technology-supported, personalized learning and allow for flexible teacher-student ratios, thus allowing teachers to serve as facilitators, coaches, mentors, and tutors rather than deliverers of information. These are just a few ideas that could be implemented so that teacher leaders can help lead change because their roles and student learning are restructured in the future. Other models are also being discussed, including those highlighted in the infographic in Figure 8.2.

FIGURE 8.1   Sample Teacher Role Structure

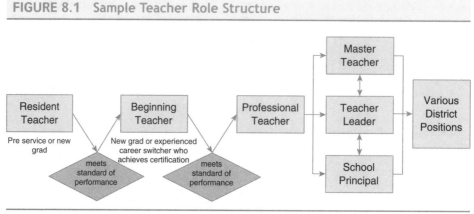

SOURCE: U. S. Department of Education (2013, p.24).

FIGURE 8.2 Teacher Leader Changing School Systems

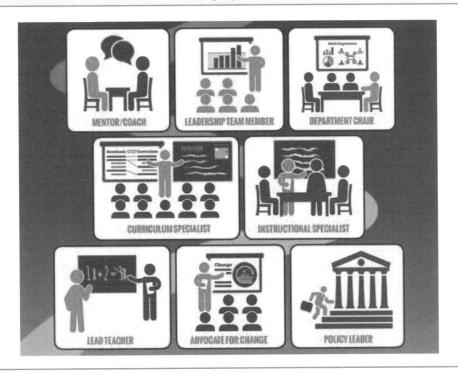

SOURCE: U. S. Department of Education (2015).

ACTIVITY: Brainstorm new or reconfigured roles for teachers and new or modified structures for instruction as you rethink teaching and organization in classrooms so that teacher leaders might have time for their efforts. Which idea seems most possible to try in your context? What idea(s) do you think would be worth piloting to see how they might actually work? A pilot project could be tried for one quarter, rather than an entire year, and then evaluated. What would be the first steps if you were to conduct a needs assessment or begin an action research project?

Recently, the DOE partnered with the NBPTS (nbpts.org), ASCD, and over 100 other supporting organizations on a project called Teach to Lead (teachtolead .org). Their goal is to engage teachers in reimaging education by encouraging cultural and policy changes that support and expand teacher leadership. With additional goals that include ensuring student achievement and keeping teachers in classrooms, this initiative also seeks to create a culture where teachers have a real say in the policies that affect their work. Such efforts to hear from teachers and tap into their knowledge and experience is critical for the future of teacher leadership given that 69% of teachers feel their opinions about decisions to be made are heard in their school, but only 32% say their opinions are heard and valued at the district level, and only 5% say this is the true at the state level, and 2% at the national level (Scholastic and the Bill & Melinda Gates Foundation, 2013). Hearing from teachers is important because job satisfaction is closely tied to how much teachers feel their voices are heard.

The DOE understands the consequences of not involving teachers in their efforts to create change. As a result, it is making an effort to listen to teachers and share the stories of states and districts that are supporting teacher leadership. It is also looking at new models for teacher leadership in the future and encouraging stakeholders at all levels to commit to expanding teacher leadership. The Teach to Lead program, for example, has sponsored several regional Teacher Leadership Summits and district- or school-based Teacher Leadership Labs to work on issues by sharing ideas and best practices, identifying challenges, generating potential solutions, and creating action agendas. The DOE has also financed Teacher Ambassadors to come to Washington to advise them for a time and offered incentives to states to help advance their teacher leadership projects. In fact, many states are also taking steps to include and support teachers as leaders in a variety of ways. Several states are "dip-ping their toes into the water" based on successful efforts in some of their districts.

> Several leading States are investing in teacher leadership as a core strat-egy to improve their educational systems. Federal programs, such as Race to the Top and the Teacher Incentive Fund, have also been catalysts for creating more teacher leadership opportunities. For example, 13 of the 19 Race to the Top states either have in place or have proposed new policies that would create roles to encourage teachers to lead while remaining in the classroom. Policies include comprehensive teacher career advance-ment initiatives, multitiered certification systems with tiers for advanced or master teachers, and certification endorsements related to teacher leadership. (U.S. Department of Education, 2015, n.p.)

Clearly, teacher leadership is a hot topic, and several states are addressing teacher leadership by designating funds and making good use of their human capital in the form of teachers serving on advisory boards to look at options for their state. For example,

- In Delaware and Hawaii teachers are participating in extended PLC times to analyze and use a variety of data to adjust their instruction to better meet the needs of their students. To support this effort, Delaware used some of its Race to the Top funding to hire coaches in each of its 237 schools to help teachers become more adept at using student data to focus their instruction on the concepts and skills that their children needed.

- Project SUCCESS in Massachusetts trains experienced teachers to become Lead Mentors for new teachers, especially in high-need schools and disciplines.

- **North Carolina** recently reallocated Race to the Top funding to create the Governor's Teachers Network, which supported the efforts of 450 teacher leaders to create and offer professional development, or to develop standards-based lesson and unit plans with formative assessments to share with their colleagues and students. Teachers in this network remained in their classrooms but earned an additional $10,000 for their efforts.

- The **Ohio** Department of Education (ODE) used part of its Race to the Top funds to hire 50 teachers to write curricula aligned with the Common Core math and English language arts standards, develop formative assessments, train teachers, and redesign teacher evaluation and feedback systems. These teachers also advised how the state's policies were affecting their schools and classrooms and helped their colleagues understand and adjust to changes in the curriculum.

- In **Tennessee,** the Teacher Leader Council developed six different teacher leader models to address implementation strategies related to the Common Core standards and Response to Intervention (RtI), as well as teacher evaluation, all with the goal of increasing teacher effectiveness and improving student achievement. These models vary with regard to the roles and compensation (monetary and/or flex time) for selected teacher leaders who may remain in their schools or not, depending on the model.

Everything we have described so far suggests growth is the immediate future of teacher leadership. Many initiatives are underway across the country, and educators at all levels are realizing the need for creating opportunities for, preparing, and supporting teacher leaders. These possibilities lead us to consider what could be accomplished with strong teacher leadership in our schools.

WHAT CAN SCHOOLS ACCOMPLISH WITH STRONG TEACHER LEADERSHIP?

In the Henry County Schools in Tennessee, they believe that teacher leadership is not a position; they see teacher leadership as an action (Tennessee Department of Education, 2014). This makes us wonder what could be accomplished if more teachers took action and stepped up as teacher leaders? To partially answer this question, we share some of the leadership projects accomplished by teachers we have worked with and share what other teacher leaders around the country are accomplishing when they take action. Here are some typical examples of what can be accomplished with strong teacher leadership:

- Teacher leaders are working to develop common formative assessments and benchmark tests in many schools, districts, and even states.

Then they collaborate with other teachers to interpret and make use of the assessment data they collect.

- Teacher leaders are developing curriculum, units and lessons, pacing guides, and instructional strategies for implementing standards-based curriculum, including the Common Core standards or other state-based standards used in many districts and states.

- Many teacher leaders are planning and delivering professional development for other teachers, saving their schools and districts many thousands of dollars. The National Writing Project (NWP) has used this model of professional learning with teachers teaching teachers for decades. It is a proven model for schools and districts that recognizes the knowledge, skills, and experience teachers have to share.

- A growing number of teachers are leading by writing blogs and creating websites to share their expertise and ideas with other teachers. Teachers all over the country read teacher-created blogs and websites for new ideas, advice and support, and even for validation and empowerment. Other teacher leaders are using Twitter and Instagram to share ideas and resources. For tech-savvy teachers, using the Internet as a resource comes naturally and is their preferred way of both communicating and learning. Many teachers are creating their own Personal Learning Networks by engaging with or following other teacher leaders on the Internet. This is true for school leaders as well.

- Many teachers show leadership by mentoring other teachers, whether they do this formally and are trained and paid for doing it, or whether they do it informally by serving as a buddy, by being a role model, or by being a confidante and providing a strong shoulder.

- More and more teacher leaders are convening and attending "unconferences" and edCamps (edcamp.org) where they can network and learn from each other. Participant-driven and highly collaborative, edCamps are available all over the world to teachers at no cost. They are a great example of crowdsourcing for teachers, and they take advantage of social networking to communicate and grow. Over 50,000 teachers have attended more than 1,000 teacher-led edCamps since 2010.

- Many teacher leaders are working with parents and other teachers to find the best ways to increase parent involvement in their particular contexts. They know that one size does not fit all when it comes to increasing parent involvement, so their efforts are often local. Teacher leaders do everything from attending parent-teacher organization meetings, to offering parent curriculum nights at their schools, to partnering with parents on school committees, to helping other teachers learn how to work well with the parents at their school.

- More and more teachers are expressing leadership by contributing videos of their classroom instruction to websites like the Teaching Channel, TeacherTube, and Vimeo so that other teachers, especially preservice and novice teachers, can learn from them.

- In a similar vein, a multitude of teachers are sharing their favorite teaching resources on Pinterest, Delicious, and LiveBinders, although they probably do not see this as a form of teacher leadership. And many teachers are making their Prezi presentations public or doing the same with other websites such as Animoto, Authorstream, Glogster, Mentormob, and Quia, to name just a few!

We also want to share some selected projects completed by participants in the TLI we described above. These capstone projects required teacher leaders to take direct action on a leadership challenge they identified and were passionate about. Their projects had to be authentic to their teaching context, have specific objectives, be doable, and have a clear beginning and end. These examples of teacher leadership reveal more of the many things that can be accomplished with strong teacher leadership.

- Creating teacher-led professional development in literacy that can be used as a model districtwide and among local associations to engage more members

- Building a coalition among the state association, local parent groups, and administration organizations to advocate for effective education legislation

- Designing a quarterly after-school Science Day for elementary school students

- Constructing a 2-year course for high school juniors and seniors that teaches social and character skill development within a project-based and discussion curriculum

- Implementing a dual enrollment Spanish classroom and increasing the number of students who earn college credits and enroll in higher education classes

- Developing a plan to help students master academic language and overcome the language gap

- Establishing a mentoring group for African-American female students who have been identified as having low self-esteem or issues with bullying

- Providing access to classes with professional musicians for students who cannot afford private lessons

- Incorporating a districtwide restorative justice approach for behavior and attendance issues

- Creating a statewide alternative curriculum for students on extended absences (approved, home-hospital, or suspensions) to ensure student access to a standardized curriculum

- Providing teachers with opportunities to participate in observational rounds on campus and learn from others' best practices

- Creating professional development on how to integrate students with emotional and behavioral disturbances into general education settings

- Creating a PLC and support group for science teachers so they can advocate for and share best practices of the Next Generation Science Standards and model successful science lessons, plans, and pedagogies

- Recruiting a district cohort that supports teachers going through the National Board Certification process with face-to-face feedback, release time, and professional development

- Investigating ways of rethinking teaching schedules and advocating for a half day each month where students are released early so teachers can collaborate to strengthen their instructional practice

- Researching the need for arts curriculum, media specialists, and guidance counselors and advocating against state legislation that proposes eliminating mandatory arts time from the curriculum

- Developing an educator leadership training model that can be effectively implemented by teachers and administrators

- Advocating for legislation that requires culturally relevant, effective multilingual instruction via advocacy with teacher organizations and policymakers

- A growing number of teacher leaders are calling for "teacher-powered schools" (see www.teacherpowered.org or www.teachingquality.org/teacherpowered) and working to make this happen

WHAT CAN SCHOOL AND DISTRICT LEADERS DO TO SUPPORT TEACHER LEADERSHIP?

To support teacher leaders, administrators need to build a strong culture for teacher leadership in their schools and district. Addressing teacher leadership on many levels and using a systems-thinking approach can help accomplish this. Just appointing teachers to formal teacher leadership roles or encouraging informal teacher leadership may be a place to start, but without a comprehensive, well-developed plan, the real power of teacher leadership will not be achieved. Building relationships, communicating, and collaborating are key elements that school and district leaders must employ wholeheartedly to build and sustain a culture of teacher leadership.

School leaders are essential in building a culture of teacher leadership. To build a culture for and sustain teacher leadership, the first step is to establish a vision for teacher leadership in any school and/or district. However, this must be done collaboratively with input and buy-in from all stakeholders. Teacher leadership cannot be mandated from the top; it needs to also be encouraged and cultivated from the bottom up. Therefore, an important step is to build partnerships with people who have experience with and expertise to share about leadership. This must include teachers who are already leading in many ways, and it should include parents and others, including those from local colleges or universities, businesses, industry, local government, or other community members. No one person can make teacher leadership happen alone. With representatives of all stakeholders at the table, the vision must be fine-tuned and then operationalized through agreed upon goals and objectives that come with benchmarks and resources to make them happen. This means that there needs to be serious discussion about funding, including finding forms of compensation and reward for the time that teacher leaders put in—financial or otherwise. Funding discussions should be transparent and should include support for professional learning opportunities for current and prospective teacher leaders. There also needs to be a plan for communicating the vision, goals, objectives, and benchmarks to everyone in the school or district. All communications about teacher leadership must convey the value and potential outcomes of the teacher leadership initiative. It is also important to communicate how all teachers can access opportunities for learning about teacher leadership and the possibilities for engaging in ways that make the most sense for their interests, talents, skills, and available time. If school or district leaders make the mistake of appointing teacher leaders rather than encouraging all with an interest, they will stymie the acceptance of appointed teacher leaders by others. Of course, school and district leaders can and should encourage teachers who have shown promise as leaders, but they must not make this an exclusive club for only the chosen few or only for the most experienced teachers. This would be a mistake that would severely restrict the development of a culture and climate of teacher leadership.

Even if teachers are not ready or interested in teacher leadership, much less in collectively running a teacher-powered school, a school with a plan for developing and supporting strong teacher leadership will benefit everyone. And the more autonomy and greater sense of individual and collective efficacy that teachers in a school have, the more likely administrators will be able to solve their teacher retention problems. It all starts with a vision and a collaboratively developed plan that is funded to develop and support a culture of strong teacher leadership.

Once the vision is enacted, it is important for school and district leaders to continue to support their teacher leaders, build their leadership skills, acknowledge their efforts in small and large ways, and respect changes in their need, availability, and desire to lead. In other words, part of the culture of teachers leading should include respecting the fact that not everyone has the time to lead outside of the school day, perhaps because they have family matters to consider. Therefore, any plan for building a culture of teacher leadership should include a wide variety of opportunities to lead so that everyone can find a way to lead. One way to make this happen is to educate teachers about what teacher leadership is and could be.

WHAT ARE SOME PROFESSIONAL DEVELOPMENT MODELS FOR PREPARING MORE TEACHER LEADERS?

If the goal is to develop strong teacher leaders, how might this be accomplished? We suggest two ways to begin this process based on the content in this book. While we do not recommend short-term PD, such as 2-hour sessions after school, we do recommend a series of half-day and full-day learning opportunities for developing teacher leaders. We also recommend an intensive 4-day summer workshop followed up with half-day or full-day sessions for teacher leaders to continue developing the knowledge and skills they need. These learning opportunities should, of course, include assignments and practical application opportunities for all who attend so that what is learned is tried out in the real world. We leave the structure of teacher leadership PD up to those charged with leading it—hopefully teacher leaders themselves—but in keeping with our discussion in Chapter 7 of the importance of conducting a needs assessment before beginning any project, here are some questions we think need to be asked and answered by an inclusive group of stakeholders before planning PD for teacher leaders:

- How was the need for teacher leadership initiated? Is it necessary? Why or why not?

- What does the school and/or district want to achieve through its teacher leadership initiative?

- What would be the ideal outcome of developing teacher leaders in the school and/or district?

- What does the school and/or district already have in place regarding teacher leadership?

- How has the school and/or district successfully initiated new ideas, programs, or approaches in the past?

- What resources are available to support teacher leadership?

- What assets could local school and/or district teachers, administrators, other staff, parents, students, community members, and business/industry or college/university partners bring to a teacher leadership initiative?

- What obstacles might hinder a successful teacher leadership initiative? How could those obstacles be overcome?

Once these questions are discussed fully, it will be time to do some planning. In Table 8.1, we recommend topics and activities for eight half-day and eight full-day sessions based on the content provided in this book. However, we believe each school or district should tailor its plans for professional learning based on its vision and goals for its own teacher leadership initiative.

TABLE 8.1 Sample Half-Day and Full-Day Professional Learning Opportunities for Teacher Leaders

OPTIONAL PLANS	SUGGESTED HALF-DAY PLANS FOR LEARNING ABOUT TEACHER LEADERSHIP	SUGGESTED FULL-DAY PLANS FOR LEARNING ABOUT TEACHER LEADERSHIP
Possible Scenarios	School with a large percentage of early career teachers, two curriculum facilitators, an assistant principal, principal, and six grade-level/team/department chairs. Up to 15 teachers who volunteer for half-day sessions about teacher leadership on early release days.	District with a similar percentage of early career, mid-career, and veteran teachers, and two central office personnel interested in coleading a teacher leadership initiative. Up to 25 teachers who volunteer for a 4-day summer workshop, followed by four more full-day sessions during autumn (or for eight full-day sessions offered monthly throughout the school year).
Goals	• To assess interest in and readiness for teacher leadership. • To learn and practice basic skills for teacher leadership. • To build a school culture that capitalizes on multiple opportunities for formal and informal teacher leadership. • Read Chapter 1 before first session.	• To build a district culture that capitalizes on multiple forms of formal and informal teacher leadership in each building. • To learn and practice basic and advanced skills for teacher leadership. • To create unique plans for teacher leadership in each school that includes professional learning experiences about teacher leadership for all teachers. • Read Chapter 1 before first summer session.
	ACTIVITIES FOR HALF-DAY SESSIONS	ACTIVITIES FOR FULL-DAY SESSIONS
Session 1	• Introduce goals and purposes of this learning opportunity. • Participants share current and past leadership experiences both in and out of school to recognize and validate that participants' already have leadership experience. • Develop a shared definition of teacher leadership. • Unpack the Teacher Leader Model Standards (see Table 1.3) by describing concrete examples for what each standard would look like in action.	• Introduce goals and purposes of this learning opportunity. • Participants share current and past leadership experiences both in and out of school to recognize and validate that participants already have leadership experience. • Presentation about various definitions and models for teacher leadership. Also, unpack the Model Teacher Leader Standards (see Table 1.3). • Participants collaboratively generate a list of knowledge, skills, and dispositions needed by teacher leaders. • Participants use the Model Teacher Leader Standards to set short-term and long-term goals for personal development as teacher leaders.

(Continued)

TABLE 8.1 (Continued)

ACTIVITIES FOR HALF-DAY SESSIONS	ACTIVITIES FOR FULL-DAY SESSIONS
• Generate a list of needed knowledge and skills for teacher leaders; prioritize the list for this group. • Read Chapter 2 for next session.	• Group develops by consensus a prioritized list of what they want to learn about teacher leadership. • Participants complete Appendix A to assess their school's culture and readiness for teacher leadership. • Participants agree on a plan for gathering data at their respective schools about the culture and readiness for teacher leadership (see also Table 2.2). • Small-group discussion of scenarios and/or complete one or more activities related to Chapter 1 (see online guidebook). • Expectations for carrying out a leadership project explained. • Read Chapter 2 and two articles listed in the online guide for Chapter 2 for next session.
Session 2	

• Discuss these questions:
  o Why do we need teacher leaders?
  o What is included in the range of things that teacher leaders do?
  o What facilitates and nurtures teacher leadership?
  o What hinders or stifles teacher leadership?
  o What could be done to overcome obstacles to teacher leadership?
• Brainstorm the knowledge, skills, and dispositions needed by teacher leaders.
• Participants each list knowledge, skills, and dispositions they currently possess (strengths) and those they wish to develop (goals).
• Read Chapter 3 for next session.
	• Participants each list knowledge, skills, and dispositions they currently possess (strengths) and those they wish to develop (goals).
	• Discuss these questions:
	  o Why do we need teacher leaders?
	  o What is included in the range of things that teacher leaders do?
	  o What facilitates and nurtures teacher leadership?
	• Create a T-chart using one column to list what hinders or stifles teacher leadership, and the other column to list what can be done to overcome obstacles to teacher leadership. Refer to readings in the online guide for Chapter 2 during this activity.
	• Brainstorm tangible and intangible rewards for teacher leaders. Have participants select what would be the best rewards for them and choose at least one idea to initiate at their school.
	• Engage in role plays or have small group discussions about the scenarios in the online guide for Chapter 2, and/or complete one or more activities in the online guide for Chapter 2.
	• Presentation on leadership styles followed by discussion of what teacher leaders need from school leaders and strategies for getting their needs met.
	• Cocreate a vision for teacher leadership that can later be adopted or modified for each school.
	• Compare data from Appendix A and/or Table 2.2 about stronger and weaker aspects of each school's culture and different levels of readiness for teacher leadership.
	• Brainstorm ideas for possible projects to improve the culture and climate for teacher leadership at

ACTIVITIES FOR HALF-DAY SESSIONS	ACTIVITIES FOR FULL-DAY SESSIONS
	each school based on results from Appendix A and other information.
	• Read Chapter 3 and suggested articles in the online guide for Chapter 3. Assign one participant to lead discussion of each assigned reading.
Session 3 • Draw and share an image or write a metaphor for yourself as a teacher leader. • Discuss your personal vision for both formal and informal teacher leadership. • Use a T-chart to list obstacles to teacher leadership and potential solutions for each obstacle. • Learn more about how metacognition helps teacher leaders. • Establish your goals as a teacher leader for the next 1, 5, and 10 years. • Read Chapter 4 for next session.	• Teacher-led discussions of readings assigned for this session. • Revisit T-chart about obstacles to teacher leadership and expand on possible solutions. Add a third column to list dispositions needed to carry out solutions. • Cocreate a (generic or specific) job description for teacher leaders that includes necessary and desirable dispositions, as well as necessary and desirable knowledge and skills. • Brainstorm criteria for a district- and schoolwide award for teacher leadership, plus a plan to initiate this award in their school. • Draw and share an image or write a metaphor for yourself as a teacher leader. • Presentation about metacognition for teacher leaders. • Draw a timeline to display your goals as a teacher leader for the next 1, 5, and 10 years. • Engage in role plays or have small group discussions of scenarios in the online guide for Chapter 3, and/or complete one or more activities in the online guide for Chapter 3. • Ask participants to update their resumes to include their dispositions, personal vision, goals, and experiences as teacher leaders. • Read Chapter 4 and suggested articles in the online guide for Chapter 4. Assign one participant to lead discussion of each assigned reading.
Session 4 • Discuss your strongly held beliefs about teaching, learning, students, curriculum, instruction, the purpose of education, leadership, and so on. • Revisit and update your goals from last session. • Learn more about the needs of adult learners from different generations. • Create a list of tips for working with adults and with different generations of teachers. • Read Chapter 5 for next session.	• Assess your metacognitive skills using Table 4.1. • Teacher-led discussions of readings assigned for this session. • Discuss the role of implicit and explicit beliefs that teachers hold; explain more about PPTs and the personal theorizing process as described in Chapter 4. • Write about your strongly-held beliefs (aka PPTs) about teaching, learning, students, curriculum, instruction, the purpose of education, and leadership for next session. Be prepared to share. • Share updated resumés. • Presentation about the needs of adult learners from different generations. • Create a specific list of tips for working with each generation of teachers.

(Continued)

TABLE 8.1 (Continued)

	ACTIVITIES FOR HALF-DAY SESSIONS	ACTIVITIES FOR FULL-DAY SESSIONS
		• Engage in role plays or have small group discussions of scenarios in the online guide for Chapter 4 and/or complete one or more activities in the online guide for Chapter 4. • Continue discussing possible leadership projects. • Read Chapter 5 and articles suggested in the online guide for Chapter 5 for next session. Assign one participant to lead discussion of each assigned reading.
Session 5	• Learn more about change theory and systems thinking. • Brainstorm ways to improve your school's climate or culture. Choose one thing to try immediately. • Coconstruct an action plan to gather feedback about your school's general readiness for teacher leadership from all constituents before next session. • Read Chapter 6 for next session.	• Guest speaker about educational policymaking in your region or state. • Teacher-led discussions of readings assigned for this session. • Focused discussion on parent and family involvement. Emphasize taking a strength-based approach to finding viable solutions. • Share successes and brainstorm ideas for making improvements in parent/family involvement in your school and/or district based on Tables 5.2 and 5.3. • Learn about change theory and systems thinking. • Engage in role plays or have small group discussions of scenarios in the online guide for Chapter 5, and/or complete one or more activities in the online guide for Chapter 5. • Revisit ways to improve your school's climate or culture in general, and regarding teacher leadership in particular (i.e., revisit results of Appendix A). Choose one thing to try immediately. • Guided development of action plans for a teacher research plan to address an important topic relevant for each participant's school (see Appendix B). • Read Chapter 6 for next session. Assign one participant to lead discussion of each assigned reading.
Session 6	• Share results of actions taken to improve school climate or culture. • Use role play to address common leadership scenarios and to practice (a) coaching language, (b) I-messages, and (c) conflict resolution skills. • Learn more about facilitating groups. • Brainstorm ways to improve communication in your PLC and/or faculty meetings. Choose one thing to try immediately. • Read Chapter 7 for next session.	• Share results of participants' efforts to improve school climate or culture—in general and/or regarding teacher leadership in particular. • Teacher-led discussions of readings assigned for this session. • Use role play to address common leadership scenarios and to practice (a) coaching language, (b) I-messages, and (c) conflict resolution skills. • Presentation or guest speaker on conflict resolution. • Complete and then discuss the Keirsey Temperament Sorter KTS-II (http://www.keirsey.com). • Brainstorm ways to improve communication in your PLC and/or faculty meetings. Choose one thing to try immediately. • Discuss Resource C in Katzenmeyer and Moller (2009) about strategies for finding time.

	ACTIVITIES FOR HALF-DAY SESSIONS	ACTIVITIES FOR FULL-DAY SESSIONS
		• Engage in role plays or have small group discussions of scenarios in the online guide for Chapter 6, and/or complete one or more activities from the online guide for Chapter 6.
		• Fine-tune action plans for a teacher research plan to address an important topic relevant for each participant's school.
		• Read Chapter 7 for next session. Assign one participant to lead discussion of each assigned reading.
Session 7	• Share results of actions to improve either PLC and/or faculty meetings. • Learn more about grant writing or about advocacy and outreach (let the group decide). • Use needs assessment strategies to identify steps for increasing teacher leadership in your school. • Cocreate an action plan to address teacher leadership at your school, or co-plan professional learning opportunities around teacher leadership for your school. • Read Chapter 8 for next session.	• Teacher-led discussions of readings assigned for this session. • Share results of actions to improve either PLC and/or faculty meetings. • Learn more about strategies for advocacy and outreach and grant writing. Invite a guest speaker about one or both of these topics. • Search online resources for possible grants for teachers at your school. • Cocreate a list of tips for writing grants to share with others at your schools—use Google Docs. • Collaborate in small groups to write and actually send an advocacy piece before the next session. • Engage in role plays or have small-group discussions of scenarios in the online guide for Chapter 7 and/or complete one or more activities from the online guide for Chapter 7. • Apply needs assessment strategies to refine steps for increasing teacher leadership in your school. • Use technology to plan and carry out a needs assessment about increasing teacher leadership in your school. • Read Chapter 8 for next session. Assign one participant to lead discussion of each assigned reading.
Session 8	• Develop formative assessments for your planned PD around teacher leadership at your school, or create a pre/postassessment for evaluating your action plan to increase teacher leadership at your school. • Prepare and practice an elevator speech to communicate either your action plan or PD plans. • Alternatively: Plan an unconference or edCamp focused on teacher leadership so that teachers can share and learn from each other. • Revisit and update your personal vision and your 1, 5, and 10-year goals for teacher leadership.	• Share your advocacy pieces. • Teacher-led discussions of readings assigned for this session. • Revisit and update your personal vision for teacher leadership. • Revisit and update your 1, 5, and 10-year goals for teacher leadership. • Prepare and practice an elevator speech to communicate either your action plan or PD plans. • Develop a districtwide or school-based plan for professional development for the next group of teacher leaders. • Alternatively: Plan an unconference or edCamp focused on teacher leadership so that teachers can share and learn from each other.

SUMMARY

In this chapter, we built on the previous seven chapters, acknowledging the dispositions, knowledge, and skills needed for teacher leadership as we considered the future of teacher leadership. In doing so we described several teacher leadership initiatives led by the U.S. Department of Education, the National Education Association, the National Board for Professional Teaching Standards, the Center for Teaching Quality, and also by several state departments of education. We know there are many other teacher leadership initiatives underway, but space prohibited us from enumerating them all. Instead we listed many examples of what teacher leaders are already accomplishing in their schools, districts, and states. We hope these will inspire you to act. This chapter concluded with ideas for what it might take to actually implement teacher leadership in a school or district by suggesting two agendas for professional learning as a place to begin. While we know each school and district must develop their own plans for developing teacher leaders, we hope this book will serve as a catalyst for action. Additional activities and scenarios to discuss are provided in the companion website for this book.

School Culture Review

Completing the School Culture Review offers you an opportunity to assess the current norms of your workplace, and the capacity for shared leadership. A PDF version of this document is available in the online guide that accompanies this book, and permission is granted to make multiple copies.

Rate the following key areas using the scale provided.

None	Low	Average	Above Average	High
0	1	2	3	4

1. Level of trust between teachers and other teachers	0	1	2	(3)	4
2. Level of trust between teachers and support staff	0	1	2	(3)	4
3. Level of trust between teachers and administrators	0	1	2	(3)	4
4. Level of trust between teachers and parents	0	1	2	(3)	4
5. Level of trust between teachers and students	0	1	2	(3)	4
6. Level of respect between teachers and other teachers	0	1	2	3	(4)
7. Level of respect between teachers and support staff	0	1	2	(3)	4
8. Level of respect between teachers and administrators	0	1	2	(3)	4
9. Level of respect between teachers and parents	0	1	2	(3)	4
10. Level of respect between teachers and students	0	1	2	(3)	4
11. Level of contribution to the workplace by teachers	0	1	2	3	(4)

(Continued)

(Continued)

12.	Level of contribution to the workplace by support staff	0	1	2	3	(4)
13.	Level of contribution to the workplace by administrators	0	1	2	3	(4)
14.	Level of progress toward working together as a team of educators and support personnel to solve problems	0	1	2	(3)	4
15.	Level of progress toward working together as a team of educators and support personnel to resolve conflict	0	1	2	(3)	4
16.	Level of progress toward working together as a team of educators and support personnel to manage change	0	1	2	(3)	4
17.	Level of progress toward working together as a team of educators and support personnel to grow professionally	0	1	2	(3)	4
18.	Level of progress toward working together as a team of educators and support personnel to strengthen relationships	0	1	2	(3)	4
19.	Level of progress toward working together as a team of educators and support personnel to reduce isolationism	0	1	2	(3)	4
20.	Level of collegiality (the existence of high levels of collaboration among teachers, mutual respect, shared work values, empathy toward others, respectful dialogue and debate about teaching and learning)	0	1	2	3	(4)
21.	Level of motivation among all educators and support personnel	0	1	2	(3)	4
22.	Level of sense of belonging	0	1	2	(3)	4
23.	Level of contentment with physical plant (aesthetics of building, climate control, etc.)	0	1	2	(3)	4
24.	Level of sense of obligation and duty	0	1	2	(3)	4
25.	Level of leadership distribution (tasks are delegated/distributed by formal leader)	0	1	(2)	3	4
26.	Level of opportunity to lead	0	1	(2)	3	4
27.	Level of informal leadership (willingness to initiate and/or take on responsibilities for the school)	0	1	(2)	3	4
28.	Level of focus on agreed-upon goals, objectives, and outcomes	0	1	2	(3)	4
29.	Level of stewardship (placing oneself in service to ideas, ideals, and people)	0	1	2	(3)	4
30.	Level of respect for school as a learning community	0	1	2	(3)	4
31.	Level of interest in coworkers being successful	0	1	2	(3)	4
32.	Level of substantive focus (focus on something because it is a good thing to do, regardless of the end results)	0	1	2	(3)	4
33.	Level of sense of purpose	0	1	2	(3)	4
34.	Level of accountability	0	1	(2)	3	4
35.	Level of work being meaningful and significant	0	1	2	(3)	4
36.	Level of schoolwide student achievement	0	1	(2)	3	4

EVERY TEACHER A LEADER   https://resources.corwin.com/everyteacheraleader

37. Level of cooperation among teachers and staff		0	1	2	(3)	4
38. Level of principal supporting teachers		0	1	2	(3)	4
39. Level of central office supporting teachers		0	1	2	(3)	4
40. Level of teachers supporting administrators		0	1	2	(3)	4

Total _____ (Add all numbers from statements 1–40)

0–40 Results indicate the workplace is a sterile organization. A major concentrated and coordinated effort should be initiated to improve the culture. This effort may need to be instigated by informal leaders. Goals, focal points for improvement, and desired outcomes need to be established. Deep-seated covenantal relationships are necessary to build trust and respect for coworkers. A collaborative, proactive team (which may include the entire faculty) should initiate improvement efforts.

41–79 There is some evidence that pockets of interest in leadership exist in the workplace. A blending of those workers should begin establishing a focus for improving the school culture. Workplace objectives need to be developed to pinpoint and address areas of concern. Strong, sincere covenantal relationships are crucial for a productive and successful culture. Improvement of relationships should be a primary focus.

80–119 Results reflect many worthwhile, respectable relations and activities at the workplace. There is evidence of many established community norms. Continued efforts are warranted to maintain and improve the acknowledged community culture. A collaborative effort should be initiated to address specific areas of weakness and to make those weaknesses a focal point for improvement.

110

120–160 Evidence suggests a high level of established norms exist that define the workplace as a positive community. This level of culture should be shared with other workplaces, as a model of true community, where the majority of personnel feel an obligation to contribute in a positive and consistent manner. Relationships are strong and sincere. A high level of trust and respect exists among the workers. A continued, long-term effort is needed to maintain this effective and caring culture that operates at a moral level of responsibility.

SOURCE: Dr. Doug Roby, Wright State University (2013). Reprinted with permission.

Conducting Teacher Action Research

Once you discover the heart of your research interests, all other questions will branch out from it.

(Chiseri-Strater & Sunstein, 2006, p. 26)

The goal of teacher action research is to take action based on what you learn from doing research—to make changes or find ways to modify things that are not working or not working well enough. This requires conducting systematic research in your classroom or school to improve student learning, to solve practical problems, to gain a deeper understanding of your students, or to critically examine new or common practices. During the teacher action research process, teachers and teacher leaders become reflective practitioners who exercise their metacognitive thinking skills during a cyclical process of questioning, planning, reflecting, acting, observing, reflecting, replanning, and questioning some more. To conduct teacher action research means you have to plan not only what you are going to study but also think about how and why.

Teacher action research can be conducted by teachers in their classrooms to improve their own practice, by teams of teachers working in pairs or small groups on a common problem, by larger groups in a grade level or department, or by everyone school-wide. Professional learning communities (PLCs) are ideal groups for undertaking action research collaboratively. Ideas for research can arise from classroom or school-wide concerns, a desire to help students or improve one's practice, or better understand teaching, learning, the curriculum, or students in new ways. Action research is not something done by outsiders. Rather, it is something teachers and teacher leaders undertake themselves as insiders to take action, achieve a goal, enact one of their strongly held beliefs (PPTs) more systematically, or try something that might help students at the individual classroom level, or even schoolwide.

Differences between action research and traditional educational research are highlighted below (Table B.1) because most of us have a traditional, positivistic view of research that includes collecting and analyzing only quantitative data. In our experience, teachers often want to collect quantitative assessment data, but we know from experience that interviews, observations, focus groups, teachers' journals, student work samples, videos, and other forms of qualitative data are equally valid forms of data used in teacher action research. Therefore, in this table we compare the practical and personal nature of teacher action research to the more theoretical and decontextualized nature of how most educators understand traditional research.

TABLE B.1 Comparing Traditional Educational Research to Teacher Action Research

TRADITIONAL EDUCATIONAL RESEARCH	TEACHER ACTION RESEARCH
Problem based on an implication or interpretation of a theory	Problem or question arises from a desire to improve practice
Purpose is to test hypotheses that can apply across the population	Purpose is to construct knowledge about self and situation and to take practice in new directions
Proposed actions are based on reflection on theory	Proposed actions are based on reflection upon one's own perceptions
Focus of the research is on educational theory	Focus of the research is on practice and practical theories, which are seen as a single concept
Colleagues are used as a source of theory and as critics of work	Colleagues are used as collaborators and mutual reflectors
Relationship with students is as an observer of subjects	Relationship with students is learner to learner
Successful research brings changes in universal understanding	Successful research brings understanding of self and specific situations

The following steps for doing action research can be used by teacher leaders who want to conduct their own research. These steps can also be used to lead others through the action research process.

Step 1. Identify interests, curiosities, problems, goals, or topics you may want to explore or change. Teacher action research projects can begin with educators planning ways to achieve their vision or enact one of their PPTs (see Chapters 3 and 4). Teacher action research can also start with a wish to understand something better, or with a dissatisfaction, a nagging concern, a desire to change or to refine something, a student whose needs are not being met, or a challenge, problem, or chronic issue. In fact, one teacher action research project may also lead you into another because additional curiosities and questions are raised in an initial study. Teacher researchers may consider focusing on one student, studying a small group of students, revamping one area of the curriculum, fixing a nagging problem in the classroom, trying something new, or studying the social issues in the classroom or school. In all cases, working collaboratively with other educators is desirable, though not required.

ACTIVITY: Select one or more of the following ways to help you begin to focus in on a topic for research: (a) Talk with a small group about things that puzzle, concern, or intrigue you in your setting. (b) Brainstorm 5 to 10 possible questions that interest you. (c) Choose three possible questions and write a paragraph about why these interest you. (d) Look at your vision statement and/or your PPTs and think about how you could research something you strongly believe in but actually do not enact often in your practice. (e) Look at the results of your School Culture Survey (Appendix A) for topics that need to be researched further. (f) Do some reading to learn more about possible research topics.

Step 2. Once an interest, curiosity, problem, goal, or topic has been identified, the next step is to **do some serious reading and research about the topic(s) that interest you to see what is already known about your topic** and what others say is relevant to your teacher action research topic. Doing background research is useful for getting ideas that you might try out and study in your classroom or school. Reading both research and practitioner articles can aid in developing and refining your preliminary research question(s). Reading also helps you figure out what data collection methods could be used to study your topic. Doing background research can be accomplished both before and after reflecting on particular interests, curiosities, problems, goals, or topics. Some educators want to learn what others have found to be successful *before* starting their action research projects, or they may want to compare the results of their action research with what others have found *after* they have analyzed their data. In other words, going to the research literature to learn what others have done is useful at several points in the teacher action research cycle.

ACTIVITY: Use these ideas to help with reviewing the literature: (a) Make a list of key words related to your research interest(s) and do a Google search using these key words—one at a time or in logical combinations. (b) Set a goal of finding and reading five research articles and five practitioner articles about your topic of interest. You will know if an article is research-based if there is data reported—whether the data is qualitative or quantitative in nature. Practitioner articles are more descriptive and usually include how-to examples. (c) Take extensive notes or write an annotated bibliography to keep track of the important points in everything you read. (d) Write a synthesis of what you learned from reading the research and practitioner literature. Use this synthesis as justification for the questions you want to answer in your teacher action research study.

Step 3. Develop and refine your research question(s). Action research questions that are not worth asking include those that can be answered "yes" or "no," or questions that educators can find answers to by reading the literature about their topic. Poor research questions are also ones you already know the answer to or something you just want to prove. Weak research questions are vague, have limited answers (might be only yes/no), are difficult to measure, include terms that are ambiguous, or are limited to one event. Research questions may not be answerable if you don't have access to data needed to answer them, or if they are not doable because of time constraints.

Good action research questions can take on many forms, although they are not easy to develop. Strong research questions are measurable, include looking at something from different perspectives, need multiple sources of data to answer completely, require listening to what students have to say, or include looking at yourself as a teacher. Many teacher researchers begin by asking *How? What? Why?* or *What if?* For example, if one of my personal practical theories (PPTs) is about building a stronger sense of community in my classroom, then I might ask: "How can I use morning meetings to build a sense of community in my classroom?" or "What happens to my classroom community when I use cooperative group learning activities at least once a week?" Or if my vision is for my students to understand what social justice means in the real world, I might ask: "What do the students in my school need to read and/or experience to help them better understand social justice?" or "What happens if we engage in service learning projects in our community to help others less fortunate than we are?"

ACTIVITY: To refine your research questions try one or more of these activities: (a) Write your research questions by starting with *How? What? Why?* or *What if?* (b) Rewrite your research question(s) at least five different ways before settling on what you think is best. (c) Be sure that every term in your research questions can be defined and operationalized in a way that it can be measured. For example, what do you mean by "sense of community"? How will you know if you have achieved a "stronger sense of community in your classroom" or school? How can this be measured? (d) Refine your research questions so they are precise and answerable. For example, consider refining "What happens when I use cooperative group learning activities more often to teach math?" to say "What happens when I use cooperative group learning activities (i.e., numbered heads together; pairs check; co-op) three times a week when teaching fractions to my fourth graders?" (e) Check to be sure you are not asking two research questions in one. If so, they should be separated. Consider having one overarching research question and several subquestions.

Step 4. Develop a plan of action for what, when, where, and how you can answer your research question(s). As part of the planning process, you need to decide how you are going to gather evidence to answer your research question(s), what kind of data you might collect, how you can gather these data systematically, and what kind of time frame you will follow. This level of planning is part of what sets teacher action research apart from what you do every day, because we know you are always trying out new things and trying to fix chronic problems. However, as a teacher researcher you must systematically study what you are doing by collecting evidence over time and analyzing it to look for patterns, or themes, changes, or numeric differences. Also, planning for action research means considering how you will balance the roles of researcher and teacher or teacher leader so that you can continue to do your regular job while gathering data. Such a balancing act not only requires some thought, but it also means choosing to collect data that is authentic. For example, you can easily use student data, student work samples, and both formative and summative assessments as part of the data you collect. And because you are both the teacher and the researcher, your own insights and observations are very important sources of data. However, they are also subject to bias, if left unexamined.

As part of your planning process, take time to reflect because in teacher action research you play so many roles and have to wear so many hats—sometimes simultaneously. Therefore, ask yourself: Who am I in relation to this research idea? How does my position affect the way I approach or understand my research topic? Who will be best served by my study? What are my hidden biases and assumptions? Once you have thought about these questions you can begin to think not just about limitations your teacher action research may have, but more important, about ways to reduce bias and guard against reinforcing your assumptions. For example, you can collect student data, such as surveys or student work samples or assessments, anonymously. You could also recruit others to do brief observations or interviews for you or partner with others to evaluate student work or help you interpret interview responses. There are all kinds of ways to increase the validity of your research once you have acknowledged your biases and positionality with regard to your research question(s).

ACTIVITY: Use these suggestions to aid in planning your research: (a) Create a detailed week-by-week time line for carrying out your teacher action research project. Check and revise it periodically to keep you on track. (b) Write a memo every 2 to 3 weeks that addresses questions such as: What have you accomplished to date on your teacher research project? What are you learning about your student(s) or the teacher(s) you are working with from carrying out your teacher research project? What are you learning about yourself while conducting your teacher research project? What data is producing the most useful or helpful information? What do you still have left to accomplish to complete your teacher research project? What concerns do you have, or what challenges are you encountering? How are you addressing these concerns or challenges?

Step 5. Collect several different kinds of data as evidence. Several different kinds of data should be collected for action research projects, depending on their appropriateness for answering the research question(s). Data collection should span a reasonable period of time, which depends on the questions being asked, whether something new is being implemented or changed and evaluated, as well as other practical considerations. We recommend collecting data for at least 6 to 8 weeks, and allowing several more weeks for data analysis and preparing a way to share the results. Here are some good sources of data for teacher action researchers to consider collecting:

- Student work samples, including portfolios of work
- Formative and summative assessments
- Scores on assignment rubrics
- Checklists of skills, behaviors, resources, and so on
- Other artifacts such as lesson plans, unit plans, comments written on student papers
- Student and/or parent surveys
- Individual interviews
- Small group interviews, known as focus groups
- Field notes based on your own observation
- Reflection journals—written by students and/or the teacher researcher
- Audio and/or video recordings
- Administrator, mentor, or peer observations

We ask teacher leaders we help to conduct action research to create a crosswalk that indicates what kind of data they will use to answer each research question. The goal is to include several types of data, at least three, in order to "triangulate" their results. Triangulation of data sources increases the validity of the data collected because the interpretation of one piece of data can be confirmed or disconfirmed by additional data. Triangulation can be achieved by collecting the same type of data over time (e.g., Interview 1, Interview 2, and Interview 3), or by collecting different kinds of data to answer a research question (e.g., interviews, observations, and student work samples). Table B.2 is an example of a Research Question X Data Source Crosswalk.

It is important to assure school leaders and parents/guardians that your goals are to improve things in your classroom or school. Therefore, we ask teacher researchers to let their administrator, their students, and their parents/guardians know that you are doing teacher action research and why. As long as you are not planning to publish your research, or present it at a conference, you do not need written consent from parents or guardians, or assent from your students. However, they should be informed. If you do plan to publish or present your data at a conference, then you do need to get written consent from all parties, and your school district may

TABLE B.2 Data Source Crosswalk

RESEARCH QUESTIONS	DATA SOURCE #1	DATA SOURCE #2	DATA SOURCE #3
Primary Research Question: How does co-teaching affect students in a fifth-grade math classroom?	Individual interviews with the teachers and the students	Observations (perhaps videotaped) of co-taught lessons	Pre-Postassessments from a co-taught math unit
Subquestion A: How is co-teaching perceived by the students?	Individual interviews with teachers	Focus group interviews with students	Pre-Post student surveys (anonymous)
Subquestion B: How does co-teaching affect the students' engagement during co-taught lessons?	Individual interviews with teachers and selected students	Observations (perhaps videotaped) of co-taught lessons	Focus group interviews with other teachers who co-teach
Subquestion C: In what ways does co-teaching affect students' achievement in math?	Preassessment scores for the unit	Observations (perhaps videotaped) of co-taught lessons	Postassessment scores for the unit

have a process to have this approved. Research questions should not be a secret, and being honest and transparent are ethical ways to conduct teacher action research. Nevertheless, we always recommend using pseudonyms to protect the privacy of all who participate in your research.

ACTIVITY: When preparing for data collection consider doing the following: (a) Write down any interview and focus group questions you want to ask, and try them with one or two people before starting your actual research study. (b) Do at least one observation before you begin the actual study. Use this observation to determine how you want to record your field notes. We suggest using a two-column format so that you keep your actual observation data separate from any interpretations, questions, or comments you might have while observing. (c) If you are videotaping or audiotaping, try this out, too, to be sure all your equipment is working and you are gathering the data you expect. (d) If you are using a survey or questionnaire of any kind, prepare it ahead of time and try it out on a few people to be sure they understand the questions you are asking. (e) Prepare any student assessments before you begin, and if you are using a pre-post measure to assess student growth, be sure the questions are the same so you can compare them.

Step 6. Analyze your data. Once you have collected data over a reasonable period of time, you will need to analyze your data. However, you can start analyzing data as you collect it. This starts with organizing all the data, reading through everything multiple times, and making notes to capture preliminary insights. The goal of data analysis is to look for patterns or themes that come up repeatedly in the data, to make comparisons between evidence collected at the beginning and the end of an action research study, and then to code or otherwise locate and highlight evidence that answers the research question(s). Often it helps to create charts and graphs to display the results of the data collected, and then summarize it in narrative form to answer your research question and subquestions. It is very important to make note of any unique or surprising findings, as well as to share results that are contrary to what was expected. It is also important to note if you have weak or strong evidence for answering your research questions. In all cases, teacher action research is interpretive research, so findings should be interpreted tentatively rather than stated as truth. For example, it is better to say "Co-teaching appeared to be effective for many of my students because 80% said they liked having more than one teacher who could answer their questions, and because the pre-postassessment scores increased for 75% of my students" rather than claiming "Co-teaching was effective for my students."

ACTIVITY: When analyzing data, consider any one or all of these suggestions: (a) Use tables to organize data. These tables should include one research question per row and then findings in the columns sorted by either the source of the data (e.g., interviews, observations, assessments, etc.) or by data representing patterns or themes that you see across your data sources (e.g., examples of engagement, examples of collaboration, examples of achievement, etc.). (b) If you have numerical data, for example from pre-postassessment data, or from surveys or questionnaires, it is worth putting the results into an Excel spreadsheet and then using the chart tools to display results in the most appropriate form (e.g., bar graph, line graph, pie chart, etc.).

Step 7. When it is **time to write up your findings**, we suggest you report the results of your action research project either by (a) discussing how each of the data sources answered each research question, or (b) by discussing each or the patterns or themes you detected in the data as they relate to your research questions. If there is more than one research question, answering each one in turn is an effective way to organize your report of your findings. Basically, writing up teacher action research is all about telling the story of what you undertook to study, how your research was accomplished, and what you learned. Supporting evidence in the form of scores or frequency counts and graphs is useful, but powerful quotes from your participants, anecdotes based on your observations, or other comments or descriptions of student work and/or teacher behaviors makes the data and your story come to life. The next step, after taking action(s) based on your findings, is to make any needed changes. You also need to share what was learned with others.

ACTIVITY: When writing up your teacher action research report, consider using the following headings:

Introduction

- This section should include why this research was needed/wanted, a brief description of your students/participants, and the location of your research.

- The introduction should answer these questions: What was the purpose of your research? Why was this research important? What might it offer to educators and students?

- Include a sentence that clearly states: *"The purpose of this teacher research study was to _____."*

Literature Review

- This section provides a rationale to support your research.

- The literature review should be based on a synthesis of what you read.

- It should answer these questions: What does other research say about your topic? What has other research NOT said about your topic? What might your research add to the literature?

Research Questions—and any subquestions

- Say something simple like: "The research questions that guided this study were _____ " (and then list them).

Data Collection (Setting or Context, Participants, and Data Sources can each be subheadings)

- This section should include a detailed description of each kind of data you collected, plus

  o A more detailed description of your research site/setting/context (choose which of these words you like).

  o Include a description of yourself and your roles as a teacher and researcher during your study. This is your positionality statement and the place to state any preconceptions or biases you have.

  o A more detailed description of your participants (again, even if you mentioned this in purpose statement) and an explanation of how/why you selected them.

  o A brief description of each type of data you collected.

  o This is the place to include your Research Question by Data Sources Crosswalk.

Data Analysis

- Describe clearly and succinctly how you analyzed your data, step by step, in the order you actually did this (e.g., First I _____; Then I _____; Next I _____; Finally, I _____ .).

(Continued)

(Continued)

- Tell what you did to ensure the validity of your study.

  ◦ Remember that you increased validity by collecting multiple sources of data over time, and that perhaps you asked peers to review your data, or did member checking by asking your participants to read and give you feedback on your interpretation of the data you collected from them.

Findings and Discussion

- Organize and report your findings by each research question.

  ◦ Under each research question address what each data source told you about each research question.

- This is where you can include direct quotes from your participants. If you use quotes, be sure to identify their source in a simple way that protects your participants' anonymity.

  ◦ For example: "I really liked it when we tried those new strategies you taught us. They helped me learn better." (Student A) or "I think the school is improving how it communicates with parents." (Principal)

- This is where you can include charts, graphs, or tables to display some of your findings.

- Summarize your main findings at the end of this section.

Implications

- Address the implications your research findings have for other teachers and/or for school leaders, parents, teacher education, or policymakers. You do not have to address all these audiences, so choose the ones who would benefit from knowing about your research findings.

Limitations

- This section answers the question: What would have made this a stronger study?
- Write about the potential limitations to your research findings (e.g., time, small numbers, attrition, being a novice researcher, etc.).
- Then state what you could do to strengthen the study if you had more time, participants, resources, and so on.

Conclusion

- Reflect here on (a) what you learned about your topic, (b) about yourself as a researcher, and (c) about the value of teacher research.
- Write about how your research contributes to the knowledge base for teachers/teaching and/or scholarship in education. Don't be shy—what does your research have to say to others?

- Include what you would do as a follow-up to your teacher research and/or what other teacher research questions you would like to study in the future.

References

- Include all references cited throughout the paper.

Appendices

- Include examples of data sources and permissions.

Step 8. Take action and share your results with others. Disseminating the results of action research projects is a crucial step. This may be done formally or informally, but it needs to happen. Teacher researchers should share their results with relevant groups including grade-level teams, PLCs, other teacher researchers, the school's administration, parent groups, and certainly with the students who participated in the action research process. Presentations can be formal or informal, but in most cases presenting the results using visuals (graphs, charts, photos, video, sample quotes, etc.) will help convey the results more clearly. Technology can be a useful tool in analyzing, reporting, and presenting the results of action research, so you should take advantage of all the technology tools available to you. Remember, however, to always use pseudonyms.

Step 9. Reflect on additional questions and future research. When educators analyze their data, consider what it means, and share it with others, they usually find that they have more questions, new curiosities, nagging concerns, and additional problems that are worthy of further teacher action research. This is why the action research process is cyclical with the results of one action research project typically leading to more questions, more research, and additional data collection and analysis, which may lead you to return to Step 1. In fact, this is normal; so suggesting future action research questions should be a part of reflecting on and writing about your action research project. Replicating you research again with different participants, or using what you learned to try something new and study it are legitimate ways to continue doing teacher action research. So is asking new questions and studying them.

ACTIVITY: Either during or after the time spent sharing the results of action research projects, we suggest asking the following questions as a way to reflect on and debrief the process of conducting teacher action research:

- What new interests, curiosities, problems, goals, or topics were raised as a result of conducting your action research project?

(Continued)

(Continued)

- If you were to study this same question, or a new question, what would you do differently? What would you keep the same because it worked well for you?

- What was your most effective source of data or data collection procedure? Why?

- What was the most challenging part of completing your teacher action research project? Why do you think it was so challenging? How could you overcome these challenges?

- What did you learn about yourself as an educator while doing action research? As a teacher leader? As a researcher? As a reflective practitioner?

Assessing Readiness for Changing School Culture

We think there is value in determining if your staff is ready for changes in school culture. Therefore, based on research by Melitski, Gavin, and Gavin (2010), we have developed the following questions to ascertain readiness to focus on teacher leadership, which we know will influence and be influenced by your school culture. These items can be rated either on a sliding scale (1–10) or by using a simple Likert scale like the one we have provided here. In either case, higher scores indicate readiness to adopt new initiatives and openness to change in your school climate. A PDF version of this document is available in the online guide that accompanies this book, and permission is granted to make multiple copies.

ASSESSING READINESS FOR CHANGING SCHOOL CULTURE

TO WHAT DEGREE DO YOU BELIEVE YOUR SCHOOL . . .	NOT AT ALL LIKE MY SCHOOL	SOMEWHAT LIKE MY SCHOOL	EXACTLY LIKE MY SCHOOL
1. Is well organized			
2. Has clear, reasonable goals and objectives			

(Continued)

(Continued)

TO WHAT DEGREE DO YOU BELIEVE YOUR SCHOOL . . .	NOT AT ALL LIKE MY SCHOOL	SOMEWHAT LIKE MY SCHOOL	EXACTLY LIKE MY SCHOOL
3. Is a place where decisions are made at the appropriate level			
4. Informs you adequately about issues and priorities of the organization			
5. Provides you the information you need to do your job			
6. Is a place where your leadership is receptive to ideas and suggestions			
7. Asks for your input before decisions are made			
8. Does not require a lot of bureaucracy to cut through when you want to do something			
9. Does not have a lot of regulations that no one understands			
10. Does not require several referrals to others to get an answer to a question you have			
11. Actively plans its efforts			
12. Readily receives cooperation from other parts of the school system			
13. Is a place where individuals work well together			
14. Is a place where there is a feeling of trust			
15. Has leaders who are viewed positively as attentive and approachable			
16. Is a place where you feel supported as an individual			
17. Is a place where your leadership actively builds teams			
18. Is a place where your leadership facilitates performance improvement when it is needed			
19. Is a place where your leadership engages in problem solving			
20. Is a place where most people are open to new ideas			

162   EVERY TEACHER A LEADER   https://resources.corwin.com/everyteacheraleader

REFERENCES

Ackerman, R., & Mackenzie, S. V. (2006). Uncovering teacher leadership. *Educational Leadership, 63*(8), 66–70.

Anderson, K., & Minke, K. (2007). Parent involvement in education: Toward an understanding of parents' decision making. *Journal of Education Research, 100*(5), 311–323.

Angelle, P. S. (2007). Teachers as leaders: Collaborative leadership for learning communities. *Middle School Journal, 38*(3), 54–61.

Arias, M. B., & Morillo-Campbell, M. (2008). *Promoting ELL parental involvement: Challenges in contested times.* The Great Lakes Center for Education Research & Practice. Retrieved from http://www.greatlakescenter.org/docs/Policy_Briefs?Arias_ELL.pdf

Arnsparger, A. (2008). 4GenR8tns: Succeeding with colleagues, cohorts & customers. Retrieved from http://www.generationsatwork.com/articles_succeeding.php

Auerbach, S. (2007). From moral supporters to struggling advocates: Reconceptualizing parents' role in education through the experiences of working-class families of color. *Urban Education, 42,* 250–283.

Barth, R. (2001). Teacher leader. *Phi Delta Kappan, 82*(6), 443–449.

Bass, B. M., & Riggio, R. E. (2005). *Transformational leadership* (3rd ed.). Mahwah, NJ: Lawrence Erlbaum.

Bass, B. M., & Riggio, R. E. (2008). *Transformational leadership.* Mahwah, NJ: Lawrence Erlbaum.

Baumann, J. F., & Duffy-Hester, A. M. (2001). Making sense of classroom worlds: Methodology in teacher research. In M. L. Kamil, D. B. Mosenthall, P. D. Pearson, & R. Barr (Eds.), *Handbook of reading research* (Vol. III, pp. 77–98). Mahwah, NJ: Lawrence Erlbaum.

Berliner, D. C. (1986). In pursuit of the expert pedagogue. *Educational Researcher, 15,* 5–13.

Berliner, D. C. (1988). Implications of studies of expertise in pedagogy for teacher education and evaluation. *New directions for teacher assessment: Proceedings of the 1988 Educational Testing Service Invitational Conference* (pp. 39–68). Princeton, NJ: Educational Testing Service.

Berry, B., Byrd, A., & Wieder, A. (2013). *Teacherpreneurs: Innovative leaders who lead but don't leave.* San Francisco, CA: Jossey-Bass.

Berry, B., & Teachersolutions 2030 Team. (2011). *Teaching 2030: What we must do for our students and public schools . . . now and in the future.* New York, NY: Teachers College Press.

Boudett, K., City, E., & Murnane, R. (2013). *Data wise, revised and expanded edition: A step-by-step guide to using assessment results to improve teaching and learning.* Cambridge, MA: Harvard Education Press.

Bradley-Levine, J. (2011). Using case study to examine teacher leader development. *Journal of Ethnographic and Qualitative Research, 5,* 246–267.

Brandt, R. (1998). *Powerful learning.* Alexandria, VA: Association for Curriculum and Supervision Development.

Brown, R. (2004). *School culture and organization: Lessons from research and experience.* Denver, CO: Paper for the Denver Commission on Secondary School Reform. Retrieved from http://www.dpsk12.org/pdf/culture_organization.pdf

Chiseri-Strater, E., & Sunstein, B. (2006). *What works: A practical guide for teacher research.* Portsmouth, NH: Heinemann.

Clouse, R. W., Goodin, T., Aniello, J., McDowell, N., & McDowell, D. (2013). Leadership metaphors: Developing innovative teaching strategies. *American Journal of Management, 13*(1), 79–92.

Collinson, V., & Cook, T. F. (2004). Collaborating to learn computer technology: A challenge for teachers and leaders. *Leadership and Policy in Schools, 3,* 111–133.

Cooper, C. (2009). Parent involvement, African American mothers, and the politics of educational care. *Equity and Excellence in Education, 42*(4), 379–394.

Cooper, J., He, Y., & Levin, B. B. (2011). *Developing critical cultural competence: A guide for 21st century educators.* Thousand Oaks, CA: Corwin.

Copeland, L. L., & Gray, R. C. (2002). Developing Maryland's technology education leaders for the 21st century: Technology education leadership project (TELP). *Journal of Industrial Education, 39*(3), 1–18.

Cornett, J. W. (1990). Teacher thinking about curriculum and instruction: A case study of a secondary social studies teacher. *Theory and Research in Social Education, 18,* 248–273.

Council for the Accreditation of Educator Preparation Programs. (2015, February). CAEP Accreditation Standards. Retrieved from http://caepnet.org/~/media/Files/caep/standards/caep-2013-accreditation-standards.pdf

Council of Chief State School Officers (CCSSO). (2011, April). *Interstate teacher assessment and support consortium (InTASC) model core teaching standards: A resource for state dialogue.* Washington, DC: Author.

Cox, M. (2007). Me and my shadow: A collaborative learning opportunity for improving mentoring practice. *Reflections, 9*(1), 1–19.

Crawford, P. A., Roberts, S. K., & Hickmann, R. (2010). Nurturing early childhood teachers as leaders: Long-term professional development. *Dimensions of Early Childhood, 38*(3), 31–38.

Danielson, C. (2006). *Teacher leadership that strengthens the profession.* Alexandria, VA: ASCD.

Darling-Hammond, L. (2000). Teacher quality and student achievement: A review of state policy evidence. *Educational Policy Analysis Archives, 8*(1), 1–44.

Davis, B., & Sumara, D. (2006). *Complexity and education: Inquiries into learning, teaching, and research.* Mahwah, NJ: Lawrence Erlbaum.

Dawson, C., & Rakes, G. (2003). The influence of principals' technology training on the integration of technology into schools. *Journal of Research on Technology in Education, 36*(1), 29–49.

Deal, T. E., & Peterson, K. D. (2009). *Shaping school culture: Pitfalls, paradoxes, and promises.* San Francisco, CA: Jossey-Bass.

Duffy, G. G., Miller, S., Parsons, S., & Meloth, M. (2007). Teachers as metacognitive professionals. In D. Hacker, J. Dunlosky & A. Graesser (Eds.), *Handbook of metacognition in Education* (pp. 240–256). Mahwah, NJ: Lawrence Erlbaum.

Easton, K. B. (2002). How the tuning protocol works. *Educational Leadership, 59*(6), 28–30.

Epstein, J. L. (1995). School/family/community partnerships: Caring for the children we share. *Phi Delta Kappan, 76,* 701–712.

Epstein, J. L. (2001). *School, family, and community partnerships: Preparing educators and improving schools.* Boulder, CO: Westview Press.

Epstein, J. L. (2002). *School, family, and community partnerships: Your handbook for action.* Thousand Oaks, CA: Corwin.

Fives, H., & Buehl, M. M. (2012). Spring cleaning for the "messy" construct of teachers' beliefs: What are they? Which have been examined? What can they tell us? In K. R. Harris, S. Graham, T. Urdan, S. Graham, J. M. Royer, & M. Zeidner (Eds.), *APA educational psychology handbook: Individual differences and cultural and contextual factors* (Vol. 2, pp. 471–499). Washington, DC: American Psychological Association.

Fullan, M. (2001). *Leading in a culture of change.* San Francisco, CA: Jossey-Bass.

Fuller, F. (1969). Concerns of teachers: A developmental conceptualization. *American Educational Research Journal, 6,* 207–226.

Fuller, F., & Brown, O. (1975). Becoming a teacher. In K. Ryan (Ed.), *Teacher education* (74th *Yearbook of the National Society for the Study of Education* (Part 2, pp. 25–52). Chicago, IL: University of Chicago Press.

Gall, M. D., Gall, J. P., & Borg, W. R. (2003). *Educational research: An introduction* (7th ed.). Boston, MA: Allyn & Bacon.

Guskey, T. R. (2014). Planning professional learning. *Educational Leadership, 71*(8), 11–16.

Hammerness, K., Darling-Hammond, L., Bransford, J., with D. Berliner, M. Cochran-Smith, M. McDonald, & K. Zeichner. (2005). How teachers learn and develop. In L. Darling-Hammond & J. Bransford (Eds.), *Preparing teachers for a changing world* (pp. 358–389). San Francisco, CA: Jossey-Bass.

Hanuscin, D. L., Rebello, C. M., & Sinha, S. (2012). Supporting the development of science teacher leaders—where do we begin? *Science Educator, 21*(1), 12–18.

Harris, A. (2003). Teacher leadership as distributed leadership: Heresy, fantasy, or possibility? *School Leadership and Management, 23,* 313–324.

Hatch, T., White, M., & Faigenbaum, D. (2005). Expertise, credibility, and influence: How teachers can influence policy, advance research, and improve performance. *Teachers College Record, 107,* 1004–1035.

Hattie, H. (2015). High impact leadership. *Educational Leadership, 72*(5), 36–40.

Hattie, J. (2009). *Visible learning: A synthesis of over 800 meta-analyses relating to achievement.* New York, NY: Routledge.

Helterbran, V. R. (2010). Teacher leadership: Overcoming 'I am just a teacher' syndrome. *Education, 131*(2), 363–371.

Henderson, A., & Mapp, K. (2002). *A new wave of evidence: The impact of school, family, and community connections on student achievement.* Austin, TX: National Center for Family and Community Connections with Schools.

Hord, S. M., Rutherford, W. L., Huling-Austin, L., & Hall, G. E. (1987). *Taking charge of change.* Alexandria, VA: Association of Supervision and Curriculum Development.

Hughes, T., & Fiehl, S. (2013, October). Talking 'bout my generation. *Inside learning technologies and skills* (pp. 45–46). Sussex, England: CloserStill.

Jackson, T., Burrus, J., Barrett, K., & Roberts, R. D. (2010). *Teacher leadership: An assessment framework for an emerging area of professional practice.* Princeton, NJ: Center for New Constructs, Educational Testing Service.

Kagan, D. M. (1992). Implications for research on teacher belief. *Educational Psychologist, 27*, 65–90.

Katzenmeyer, M., & Moller, G. (2009). *Awakening the sleeping giant: Helping teachers develop as leaders* (3rd ed.). Thousand Oaks, CA: Corwin.

Kemmis, S., & McTaggart, R. (Eds.). (1988). *The action research planner* (3rd. ed.). Geelong, Victoria, Australia: Deakin University Press.

Knowles, M. (1980). *The modern practice of adult education: From pedagogy to andragogy* (2nd ed.). Englewood Cliffs, NJ: Prentice Hall/Cambridge.

Kurtts, S., & Levin, B. B. (2000). Using peer coaching with preservice teachers to develop reflective practice and peer support. *Journal of Research in Education, 11*, 297–310.

Larocque, M., Kleiman, I., & Darling, S. M. (2011). Parental involvement: The missing link in school achievement. *Preventing School Failure, 55*(3), 115–122.

Leithwood, K., Jantzi, D., & McElheron-Hopkins, C. (2006). The development and testing of a school improvement model. *School Effectiveness and School Improvement, 17*(4), 441–464.

Levin, B. B. (2003). *Case studies of teacher development: An in-depth look at how thinking about pedagogy develops over time.* Mahwah, NJ: Lawrence Erlbaum.

Levin, B. B. (2014). The development of teachers' beliefs. In H. Fives & M. G. Gill (Eds.), *International handbook of research on teachers' beliefs* (pp. 48–65). New York, NY: Taylor & Francis/Routledge.

Levin, B. B., & Schrum, L. (2012). *Leading technology-rich schools: Award-winning models for success.* New York, NY: Teachers College Press.

Lieberman, A. (2011). Can teachers really be leaders? *Kappa Delta Pi Record, 48*(1), 16–18.

Little, J. W. (2003). Constructions of teacher leadership in three periods of policy and reform activism. *School Leadership and Management, 23*, 401–419.

Louis, K. S., & Wahlstrom, K. (2011). Principals as cultural leaders. *Phi Delta Kappan, 92*(5), 52–56.

Lundeberg, M. A., & Levin, B. B. (2003). Prompting the development of preservice teachers' beliefs through cases, action research, problem-based learning and technology. In J. Raths & A. McAninch (Eds.), *Teacher beliefs and teacher education. Advances in teacher education* (Vol. 6, pp. 23–42). Charlotte, NC: Information Age.

Lytle, S., & Cochran-Smith, M. S. (1990). Learning from teacher research: A working typology. *Teachers College Record, 92*(1), 83–103.

MacNeil, A. J., Prater, D. L., & Busch, S. (2009). The effects of school culture and climate on student achievement. *International Journal of Leadership in Education, 12*, 73–84.

Margolis, J., & Deuel, A. (2009). Teacher leaders in action: Motivation, morality, and money. *Leadership & Policy in Schools, 8*(3), 264–286.

Mayrowetz, D. (2008). Making sense of distributed leadership: Exploring the multiple usages of the concept in the field. *Educational Administration Quarterly, 44*(3), 424–435. doi: 10.1177/0013161X07309480

McDonald, J. P., Mohr, N., Dichter, A., & McDonald, E. C. (2013). *The power of protocols: An educator's guide to better practice* (3rd ed.). New York, NY: Teachers College Press.

McQuillin, S. D., Straight, G. G., & Saeki, E. (2015). Program support and value of training in mentors' satisfaction and anticipated continuation of school-based mentoring relationships, mentoring & tutoring: Partnership in learning. *Mentoring & Tutoring: Partnership in Learning, 23*(2). Published online May 29, 2015. doi: 10.1080/1361 1267.2015.1047630

Melitski, J., Gavin, D., & Gavin, J. (2010). Technology adoption and organizational culture in public organization. *International Journal of Organization Theory and Behavior, 13*, 546–568.

Merriam, S. B., Caffarella, R., & Baumgartner, L. (2007). *Learning in adulthood: A comprehensive guide* (3rd ed.). San Francisco, CA: Jossey-Bass.

MetLife. (2013). Metropolitan Life survey of the American teacher: Challenges for school leadership. Retrieved from https://www.metlife.com/assets/cao/foundation/MetLife-Teacher-Survey-2012.pdf

Moll, L. C., & Greenberg, J. M. (1990). Creating zones of possibilities: Combining social constructs for instruction. In L. C. Moll (Ed.), *Vygotsky and education: Instructional implications and applications of sociohistorical psychology* (pp. 319–348). New York, NY: Cambridge Press.

Murphy, J., Smylieb, M., Mayrowetz, D., & Louis, K. S. (2009). The role of the principal in fostering the development of distributed leadership. *School Leadership and Management, 29*(2), 181–214.

Nussbaum-Beach, S. (2007). Teacher as leader. Retrieved from http://21stcenturylearning.typepad.com/blog/2007/02/teacher_as_lead.html

Oberg, A., & McCutcheon, G. (1987). Teachers' experience doing action research. *Peabody Journal of Education, 64*(2), 116–128.

Orton, J. D., & Weick, K. E. (1990). Loosely coupled systems: A reconceptualization. *Academy of Management Review, 15*(2), 203–223.

Pajares, M. F. (1992). Teacher's beliefs and educational research: Cleaning up a messy construct. *Review of Educational Research, 62*, 307–322.

Phelps, P. H. (2008). Helping teachers become leaders. *Clearing House, 81*(3), 119–12.

Pittman, K., & O'Neill, L. (2001). Using metaphors to evaluate ourselves: Tips for new teachers. *Classroom Leadership, 4*(5). Retrieved from http://www.ascd.org/publications/classroom-leadership/feb2001/Using-Metaphors-to-Evaluate-Ourselves-.aspx

Qualters, D. (2010). *A discussion guide for facilitators.* Madison, WI: Magna. For more information, go to http://www.magnapubs.com

Raffanti, M. A. (2008). Leaders "sitting beside" followers: A phenomenology of teacher leadership. *Journal of Ethnographic & Qualitative Research, 3*, 58–68.

Rice, J. K. (2003). *Teacher quality: Understanding the effectiveness of teacher attributes.* Washington, DC: Economic Policy Institute.

Richardson, V. (1996). The role of attitudes and beliefs in learning to teach. In J. Sikula (Ed.), *Handbook of research on teacher education* (pp. 102–119). New York, NY: Simon & Schuster/Macmillan.

Richardson, V. (2003). Preservice teachers' beliefs. In J. Raths & A. McAninch (Eds.), *Teacher beliefs and teacher education: Advances in teacher education* (pp. 1–22). Greenwich, CT: Information Age.

Robinson, V. M., Lloyd, C. A., & Rowe, K. J. (2008). The impact of leadership on student outcomes: An analysis of the differential effects of leadership types. *Educational Administration Quarterly, 44*(5), 635–674.

Roby, D. (2011). Teacher leaders impacting school culture. *Education, 131*(4), 782–790.

Sanders, D. A., & Sanders, J. A. (1984). *Teaching creativity through metaphor: An integrated brain approach.* New York, NY: Longman.

Scholastic and the Bill & Melinda Gates Foundation. (2013). *Primary sources: America's teachers on teaching in an era of change* (3rd ed.). New York, NY: Scholastic. Retrieved from http://www.scholastic.com/primarysources/PrimarySources3rdEditionWithAppendix.pdf

Schön, D. (1983). *The reflective practitioner: How professionals think in action.* New York, NY: Basic Books.

Schön, D. (1987). *Educating the reflective practitioner: Toward a new design of teaching and learning in the professions.* San Francisco, CA: Jossey-Bass.

Schrum, L., & Levin, B. B. (2009). *Leading 21st century schools: Harnessing technology for engagement and achievement.* Thousand Oaks, CA: Corwin.

Schrum, L., & Levin, B. B. (2015). *Leading 21st century schools: Harnessing technology for engagement and achievement* (2nd ed.). Thousand Oaks, CA: Corwin.

Senge, P., Cambron-McCabe, N., Lucas, T., Smith, B., Dutton, J., & Kleiner, A. (2000). *Schools that learn.* New York, NY: Doubleday/Currency.

Shulman, L. (2004). Professional development: Learning from experience. In S. Wilson (Ed.), *The wisdom of practice: Essays on teaching, learning, and learning to teach* (pp. 503-522). San Francisco: Jossey-Bass.

Smith, J., & Wohlstetter, P. (2009). *Parent involvement in urban charter schools: A new paradigm or the status quo?* Report prepared for School Choice and Improvement: Research in State, District and Community Contexts, Vanderbilt University. Retrieved from http://www.vanderbilt.edu/schoolchoice/conference/papers/Smith%20-Wohlstetter_COMPLETE.pdf

Snyder, B. R. (1971). *The hidden curriculum.* New York, NY: Alfred A. Knopf.

Spillane, J. P. (2005). Distributed leadership. *Educational Forum, 69,* 143–150.

Spillane, J. P., Halverson, R., & Diamond, J. (2001). Investigating school leadership practice: A distributed perspective. *Educational Researcher, 30*(3), 23–28.

Teacher Leadership Exploratory Consortium. (2012). *Teacher leader model standards.* Retrieved from http://www.teacherleaderstandards.org

Tennessee Department of Education. (2014). *Worth beyond measure: Tennessee teacher leader guidebook.* Available at https://www.tn.gov/education/topic/teacher-leader-guidebook.

Tuckman, B. W. (1965). Developmental sequence in small groups. *Psychological Bulletin, 63,* 384–399.

Tuckman, B. W., & Jensen, M. C. (1977). Stages of small group development revisited. *Group and Organizational Studies, 2,* 419– 427.

U.S. Department of Education. (2012). *The RESPECT Project: Envisioning a teaching profession for the 21st century.* Washington, DC: U.S. Department of Education. Retrieved from http://www.ed.gov/teaching/national-conversation

U.S. Department of Education. (2013). *A blueprint for R.E.S.P.E.C.T.: Recognizing educational success, professional excellence, and collaborative teaching.* Washington, DC: U.S. Department of Education. Retrieved from http://www2.ed.gov/documents/respect/blueprint-for-respect.pdf

U.S. Department of Education. (2015). *Progress: Teachers, leaders, and students transforming education.* Washington, DC: U.S. Department of Education. Retrieved from http://sites.ed.gov/progress/category/teacher-and-leader-preparation-and-pathways/

Van Houtte, M., & Van Maele, D. (2011). The black box revelation: In search of conceptual clarity regarding climate and culture in school effectiveness research. *Oxford Review of Education, 37*(4), 505–524.

Verloop, N., Van Driel, J., & Meijer, P. (2001). Teacher knowledge and the knowledge base of teaching. *International Journal of Educational Research, 35*(5), 441–461.

Weick, K. E. (1976). Educational organizations as loosely coupled. *Administrative Science Quarterly, 21,* 1–19.

Wenglinsky, H. (2002). How schools matter: The link between teacher classroom practices and student academic performance. *Education Policy Analysis Archives, 10*(12), 1–30.

Wiggins, G., & McTighe, J. (2005). *Understanding by design* (expanded 2nd ed.). Alexandria, VA: Association for Supervision and Curriculum Development.

York-Barr, J., & Duke, K. (2004). What do we know about teacher leadership? Findings from two decades of scholarship. *Review of Educational Research, 74*(3), 255–316.

Zemke, R., Raines, C., & Filipczak, B. (2013). *Generations at work: Managing the clash of Boomers, Gen Xers, and Gen Yers in the workplace* (2nd ed.). New York, NY: American Management Association (AMACOM).

INDEX

Unconferences, 134
U.S. Department of Education
    encouraging teacher leadership, 129–132, 144
    policy created by, 70
University of Phoenix, 8

Van Houtte, M., 77
Van Maele, D., 77
Verbal affirmation, rewarding teacher leaders
    with, 30
Video examples, 97
Vimeo, 135

Vision
    school culture and, 77
    for teacher leadership, 40–42, 137
Visioning, 40
Voicethread, 97, 112
Volunteering, parent involvement and, 81, 82

Wahlstrom, K., 12
Web 2.0 tools, 97
Work-at-home days, rewarding teacher leaders with, 31

York-Barr, J., ix, 2

CORWIN

A SAGE Publishing Company

Helping educators make the greatest impact

CORWIN HAS ONE MISSION: to enhance education through intentional professional learning.

We build long-term relationships with our authors, educators, clients, and associations who partner with us to develop and continuously improve the best evidence-based practices that establish and support lifelong learning.

Solutions you want. Experts you trust.
Results you need.

AUTHOR CONSULTING

Author Consulting

On-site professional learning with sustainable results! Let us help you design a professional learning plan to meet the unique needs of your school or district. www.corwin.com/pd

INSTITUTES

Institutes

Corwin Institutes provide collaborative learning experiences that equip your team with tools and action plans ready for immediate implementation. www.corwin.com/institutes

ECOURSES

eCourses

Practical, flexible online professional learning designed to let you go at your own pace. www.corwin.com/ecourses

READ2EARN

Read2Earn

Did you know you can earn graduate credit for reading this book? Find out how: www.corwin.com/read2earn

Contact an account manager at (800) 831-6640 or visit **www.corwin.com** for more information.

CORWIN